Cry Freedom

Cry Freedom

Mary Pytches

New Wine Ministries

New Wine Ministries
PO Box 17
Chichester
West Sussex
United Kingdom
PO19 2AW

ISBN 978-1-905991-17-4

Typeset by CRB Associates, Reepham, Norfolk
Cover design by CCD, www.ccdgroup.co.uk
Printed in Malta

Contents

Introduction

I once talked with a young church leader who told me, "I don't know what's wrong with my life, but I always feel like I'm walking around dragging a ball and chain behind me. I want to move forward, to have everything God wants for me, but I can't get there because of this ball and chain holding me back."

In response to conversations like this I gave a series of talks at New Wine entitled "Cry Freedom". The following chapters are taken from those talks. Freedom is a huge and important subject and was promised by Jesus to His disciples when He said that if *"the Son sets you free, you will be free indeed"* (John 8:36). As we read those words our hearts leap with anticipation but quickly fall again as we face the areas of bondage we are still struggling with. Therefore, in the early chapters we look at the kind of things which tie us up in knots, and also the different steps we can take to enter into the freedom that Christ has promised us. The second half of the book is taken up with the cost of freedom. The ultimate price, of course, has been paid by Jesus. But for us to enter into what Jesus has gained for us there may be certain things we need to let go of. That may seem costly.

The book has been compiled by Tim Pettingale, who patiently listened to the CDs of all the talks. He then had the job of making sense of my spontaneous chatter and translating it from the spoken word to the written word. No easy task!

I hope that the message of freedom comes across – freedom to be all that God has designed us to be.

Cry Freedom

I regularly receive letters from people who have heard me speak at conferences or other gatherings. They write to share their reflections or comment about something I have said at a particular meeting. But some time ago I heard from a young man – I'll call him Michael – and his letter stood out as being quite different from the "normal" kind of mail I receive. It disturbed me and set me thinking seriously about the subject of "freedom" – what it means to be spiritually and emotionally "free" and to be a whole person.

Jesus makes a compelling statement In John's Gospel about freedom:

> *"If you hold to my teaching, you are really my disciples. **Then you will know the truth, and the truth will set you free."***
>
> (John 8:31–32, emphasis added)

He backs up this statement up with the words,

> *"If the Son sets you free, you will be free indeed."* (John 8:36)

Clearly, Jesus wants us to know that God's desire is for every one of us to be utterly, wonderfully *free*; to be whole people, liberated by His truth. Michael's letter reminded me that the reality for so many people, even those who have been Christians for a long time, is that they are not truly "free". My heart went out to Michael. I quote part of what he said:

> "Over the years the Lord has shown me incredible love and care. I often hear encouraging words from both the Lord and other people. I know they speak the truth. But all these words and deeds of love and care have been like water off a duck's back. It is driving me to despair, guilt and worthlessness. Added to this I have a deep sense of failure and fear of failure."

Michael has been a Christian for many years. He is a member of a loving church and over time he has received a lot of good teaching. Yet, he says that all of this was like, "water off a duck's back". In other words, the truth of God's Word has penetrated his mind, but not his heart. Instead of feeling loved and valued, he feels guilty and worthless. He says he is not experiencing the freedom Christ spoke of.

Michael is far from being alone in suffering from this condition. In his book, *Ruthless Trust*, Brennan Manning states that the biggest obstacle on his personal journey of faith has been an oppressive sense of insecurity, inadequacy, inferiority and low self-esteem. This is quite a staggering confession coming from one whom many readers will regard as an outstanding writer with a gift for expressing profound truths. Manning has followed Christ for many years, and in addition to his writing skills, he is also an excellent public speaker and communicator. Yet he speaks of his personal inferiority complex and deep insecurity.

I wonder how many of us silently struggle with the same feelings of fear, self-doubt and anxiety that Michael and Brennan Manning both speak of. I believe the problem is far more common than any of us are letting on. Here are the facts: life is difficult. We live in a fallen world surrounded by fallen people. We make mistakes and hurt others and they make mistakes and hurt us. Sometimes we intentionally wound others and are deliberately wounded in return. Beyond such relational tensions, which are part and parcel of life, there is a spiritual battle taking place that has implications for our individual and personal wholeness. Simply put, God wants us whole and Satan doesn't. In fact, the closer we move towards wholeness and freedom, the more the enemy tries to trip us up and trap us. Michael's letter has caused me to ponder on just how we can live in the freedom that Jesus talked about.

The kingdom overlap

One of the reasons we don't always experience God's power and freedom is that we are living in what others have called the "kingdom overlap". Right now God's kingdom has come among us, but it has not yet been manifest in all its fullness and glory. That will happen when Christ comes again. We have already experienced something of the kingdom of God breaking into our lives, but there is much more to come! Because of the kingdom overlap, problems will continue to plague us and from time to time we will face severe difficulties and struggles.

However, whilst recognising that we are living in this "overlap", we can still live with the expectation of seeing more than we do of God's kingdom manifested in our lives. We should expect constant breakthroughs of healings, miracles and increasing freedom in Christ. We certainly shouldn't expect to "plateau" and settle for less.

Before we explore some ways in which we can move towards a place of greater freedom in our lives, I want to differentiate between what I would term a "normal" emotional reaction to life's circumstances and the kind of fear, anxiety and self-doubt that has characterised Michael's life.

Naturally when something bad happens to us we will have an emotional reaction. Life can be difficult and we wouldn't be human if we didn't experience some painful feelings over losing a job, our health, or a loved one etc. This side of glory we may suffer moments of depression, anxiety or fear, but these experiences should never derail us in our faith, nor rob us of the freedom Jesus won for us. But I think this is different from the life-long sense of hopelessness and anxiety that Michael experiences.

So how then can we move forward and experience more of Jesus' freedom than we do now? There are a number of relevant issues to be considered that will help us to understand why we have a tendency to be emotionally and spiritually bound up.

The "soil" we are planted in

It is very helpful to understand where many of our problems come from, but the understanding in itself will not heal us. All it does is to make us more cognitive neurotics! Understanding the root of our problems, however, can give us some keys to unlocking our situation so that we can pray more effectively and find healing and help to resolve the issues we are struggling with.

My husband David and I are blessed with a lovely garden, but unfortunately neither of us are gardeners. When we first moved into our house, my friend Prue Bedwell thought she would help propagate our new garden, so for my birthday she gave me a lovely peony. I took the plant, dug a hole in a place where I would be able to see it from my study window and planted it in the ground. In its first year it produced no flowers at all and I thought, "That's sad. I wonder what I can do about it." I assumed, because that's what's done with so many other shrubs, it should be cut back. I proceeded to do so and later mentioned it to Prue. She was horrified! "You did what? Mary, that's a tree peony. You never cut a tree peony back. You've probably traumatised it!" she said.

Basically my peony has had two problems: first of all I planted it in very poor soil. I literally dropped it into the ground and covered it over. I didn't add any nutrients to the soil to help the plant to thrive. Secondly, I traumatised it by cutting it back which one is not supposed to do. No wonder the peony has struggled!

We humans are much the same. The environment into which we are born (the soil in which we are planted) is very important to our development. In an ideal world our environment would be rich and nourishing, full of the right nutrients to help us develop into healthy, well-adjusted adults. Sadly, we know only too well that this is rarely the case.

Traumatic experiences
Not only is our environment very important, what happens to us as we grow and mature has a critical effect on our development. All of us will experience trauma at some time or another. Things happen to us or around us which affect our emotional wellbeing. If we are planted in rich, nourishing soil then trauma need not cause us long-term damage. But if we have grown up in poor soil then the damage can be long lasting. My poor peony would have recovered from its trauma had its soil been of a better quality. As it is, it will take a very long time to recover and I will need to infuse its soil with nutrients to help it to flourish as it should.

It is inevitable that we will have traumatic experiences in life. Recently I was talking with a young man of about thirty who was very depressed. He told me that when he was five years old his parents, who were missionaries in Asia, brought him home to England and placed him in a boarding school. He vividly recalled the day his parents left him there before travelling back to the mission field. He was utterly distraught. When it came time to say goodbye he threw himself at their feet and clung to them, sobbing and begging them not to leave him behind. But his parents still went, believing they were following a solemn call to duty. Because they were long-term missionaries they rarely came home on furlough and this meant that he did not see them again for another five years when he was ten. The sense of loss and abandonment this caused had followed him into adulthood and it was not difficult to recognise the roots of his present condition. In those crucial developmental years he was planted in what could be described as "the poor soil of absentee parents".

What about the horrendous trauma of abuse – deliberate trauma inflicted by one human being on another? One young girl that I prayed with had been sexually abused by the lodger who lived with her family. He had been invited into the family home to rent a room and eventually everyone became so used to having him around the house that they trusted him to baby-sit their young daughter. The moment he was left alone with her, he abused her.

At a recent conference a young man told me that he had been out to dinner with his parents the night before and his father had drunk too much. It brought up painful memories of the violence he had suffered as a child. His father was an alcoholic and he never knew when his dad would come home drunk and beat his mother. As a young boy he struggled with the anguish of whether to try and rescue his mother or just stay in his room blocking out the screaming and yelling. All of these foreboding thoughts and feelings flooded back into his mind that night as he sat watching his father get drunker and drunker.

Then there is the trauma of rejection. A young man of about seventeen recently asked me to pray with him. He told me that he had tried to commit suicide a few years earlier and though that was in the past he was still very insecure and anxious. He then told me the tragic story of five years of consistent bullying he had received at the hands of boys from his school. He had been completely traumatised by what had happened to him.

The environment in which we spend our formative years has such an impact on how we handle the difficulties of life later on. Our "soil" becomes part of the very fabric of us. It forms our thinking and attitudes to life. Some of the negative effects of a dysfunctional home are:

1. Poor communication leading to a lack of healing
People can recover when bad things happen to them *if* they are planted in a good environment. God has built healing into family life. Someone has said, "The family that *feels* together, *heals* together." In situations where the family unit is able to talk together and openly discuss the problems that arise – from the trivial to the traumatic – that communication speeds recovery. Where communication is poor or non-existent, recovery is seriously impeded.

When a child experiences something bad, much healing comes by being able to come home and talk about it to someone who will listen patiently, compassionately and sympathetically. In a loving, caring environment, emotional trauma can be dealt with and resolved as it occurs. If the child has no one to talk to about what has happened then the issue remains unresolved because he/she is too immature to resolve it on their own.

I heard of one young girl who was sexually abused by a neighbour when she was seven or eight years old. She wasn't the only child in the neighbourhood to have suffered in this way and eventually the Police began making enquiries in the area. In the course of their investigations they called at her house and spoke to her mother. They asked her mother if she knew whether her daughter had had a bad experience with this neighbour. The mother turned to the little girl and asked, "Have you ever been touched by this man?" The girl broke down and poured out the story of abuse. Ignoring the policeman, her mother turned to her and said, "Don't you *ever* tell anybody about this – especially not your father." This shutdown in communication over the trauma meant that it was left unresolved and healing was not possible. Little wonder then that by the age of thirty this lady became severely depressed.

2. Basic needs are unmet

The second major effect of growing up in poor soil is that we don't get our basic needs met. It has been well documented elsewhere that each of us has three basic, overriding needs that surpass all other concerns: the need for security, significance and self-worth. Frank Lake has referred to these needs as our "foetal shopping list". The heart cry of every new baby is, "Please love me! Please help me to achieve something! Please make me feel valued!"

When these very basic needs are unmet we are left with a vacuum inside, an emotional hole crying out to be filled. A celebrated American professor of psychiatry, Dr Irvine Yalom, noticed the "emotional vacuum" phenomenon early in his career and often raised the issue at his lectures. Yalom would ask members of his audience to find a partner and ask them a simple question: "What do you want?" Yalom writes about what invariably results from this experiment:

> "Such an ordinary question, yet within moments the room is rocking with emotion. Successful, well-functioning, well-dressed people who glitter as they walk are stirred to their depths. They call out to those who are forever lost: dead or absent parents, spouses, children, friends, 'I want your love. I want to see you again. I want to know you're proud of me.' So much wanting, so much longing, so much pain so close to the surface – only minutes deep; destiny pain, existence pain, pain that is always there, whirring continuously just beneath the membrane of life." [1]

The emotional "pain" the professor describes is the outcome of upbringing in a poor environment, when a person's basic needs have been constantly ignored, or of unresolved emotional trauma. People can put on a convincing façade of being "OK", but the unresolved issues that plague them are hidden only superficially.

3. Poor modelling

People who have grown up in a negative environment with poor role models for life will often react in one of two ways. They either "copy" the behaviour of their role models and caregivers or do the exact opposite.

Brennan Manning's mother was brought up in an orphanage. She didn't receive much love and attention, so she found it extremely difficult to give adequate love and attention to her children. She suffered a dysfunctional childhood and that caused her to "recreate" a dysfunctional home environment for her own children. She lived out what for her was "normality".

What a child observes as a child he/she tends to take at face value. Even though it may be a dysfunctional home the child accepts the status quo and this robs them of understanding what is "normal". A child isn't intellectually sophisticated enough to understand that their particular experience is abnormal. They may essentially understand that something is "not as it should be", but they are at a loss to know how this happened and what to do about it. "Normal" to such a child might be a home where people don't communicate, where conflicts are never resolved, where a father comes home drunk, where a mother suffers from depression, or where a father ignores his family and has no idea how to affirm his children.

Often people will react to poor modelling by deciding to do the exact opposite. As a child I was often left in someone else's care by my parents whilst they were "busy" in the family business. At some stage I decided I didn't like my parents' approach and was determined to do the opposite, so when my children were young I rarely allowed them to be looked after by a babysitter. I couldn't bear leaving my children remembering how I had hated it. But in my anxiety I went to extremes.

The ABC of our emotions

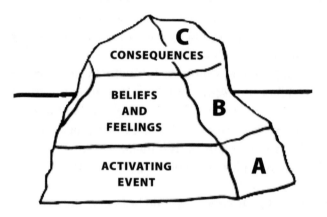

The above diagram shows the "ABC" of our emotions. This is taken from Albert Ellis' rational emotive therapy (RET). The "A" stands for Activating events, "B" for Beliefs and "C" for Consequences. The diagram depicts an iceberg, nine tenths of which is submerged beneath the water. It is a good illustration of the way people are. Our first encounter with others is usually very superficial. We have no idea what makes the person tick, what they are thinking, or what has caused their thinking. All this is like the 9/10ths of the iceberg which is submerged beneath the surface of life.

Our diagram shows that the events of life (A) causes thoughts (B) to go through our minds as a result of those events. For example, if your experience of home life as a child was that disagreements could only be resolved by having a blazing row, your attitude to conflict will have been formed as a result of that experience. Consequently, you may believe that the only way to resolve a difference of opinion is by yelling and forcing your opinion on others. Conversely, you may have come to hate conflict and so you believe that it is better to pursue peace at any price, even when it's not healthy to do so. Both of these outcomes are the result of your thinking. All of our actions (C) are based upon the beliefs (B) we hold, and these are formed from our experience of life (A).

The girl I mentioned earlier who was sexually molested by her neighbour and silenced by her mother grew up believing that the incident was her fault, that she had somehow done something terrible to cause her mother to behave as she did. Her perception of events caused her to believe that she was a "bad person". She told herself over and again, "There is something wrong with me." Notice that she didn't think, "There's something wrong with that man because of what he did to me" or "There's something wrong with my mother because she wouldn't let me talk about what happened." She internalised her pain because she was not allowed to communicate it freely and a false belief about herself was formed. Over time that unhealthy belief caused a consequence – depression and breakdown.

Similarly, Brennan Manning, not understanding why his home life was the way it was, did what any child would do – he blamed himself for it. The consequence was that he grew up believing himself to be worthless. Manning expressed his beliefs with these words: "I am a burden and an inconvenience to others. I am a failure and therefore worthless." That was the assumption he drew from his unloving and unsupportive home life.

Poor soil and trauma lead us to hold these sort of damaging beliefs. We make assumptions based on our experience, born out of immaturity. Once formed, however, these beliefs are hard to dislodge; they stick with us. Most of us have some "stuck" beliefs that we must work relentlessly to counteract. One of my false beliefs has been that I don't need other people. Such a notion came directly out of my childhood experiences. Events taught me that people are never there when you really need them. Gradually a belief formed that if people were not going to be there for me, then there was no point in needing them and I concluded that I was the only person I could depend on. This belief had consequences: I became independent and tended to keep people at arm's length. It takes time and hard work to change such an embedded belief.

Beliefs can become like "strongholds" in our lives. Many authors have referred to ungodly beliefs in this way. These are inaccurate perceptions which have resulted in attitudes to life that have become fixed in our minds. Satan does his utmost to keep us in bondage to these unhealthy ways of thinking.

So ingrained are our beliefs that we often try to justify their existence. We say to ourselves, "My beliefs aren't that irrational. People really are not to be trusted. I can prove it to you. I can show you all the people who have let me down throughout my life, therefore my belief is absolutely accurate." It sounds very plausible, but that only explains our bondage; it does not reflect our freedom in Christ. The example of Jesus shows us a different way. Jesus trusted His disciples even when they let Him down. He also spoke about loving and needing one another. He expressed our need of unity and oneness in order to function properly. So while such beliefs may seem rational to us, in fact they are not godly beliefs. Michael, who wrote to me, has a stronghold in his mind that he needs to dismantle.

Summary

There is a gap between our knowledge of the truth – what we know that Christ has won for us – and our experience of that freedom – how much we appropriate it in our lives. There are various reasons for this:

1. We live in a "kingdom overlap" amidst a fallen world where God's kingdom is not yet fully manifest in all its glory.
2. The quality of the soil we were planted in i.e. the environment in which we grew up. Many factors to do with our environment and nurturing, or lack of it, can affect our emotional freedom:
   - Traumatic experiences and how they are handled
   - Poor communication leading to a lack of healing
   - Basic needs going unmet
   - Poor examples from role models

The ABC of our emotions

The things that happen to us in life (Activating events) are instrumental in forming our Beliefs and these in turn have Consequences. Our beliefs and the events that formed them tend to be hidden below the surface of our lives. Often we form ungodly beliefs about ourselves, others or God because of negative past events. These beliefs become strongholds in our minds which need to be "overwritten" by applying biblical truth.

Notes

1. Irvin D. Yalom, *Love's Executioner*, Penguin Books, London, 1988.

The Stronghold of Ungodly Beliefs

CHAPTER

2

We saw in the previous chapter that activating events cause us to hold certain beliefs and those beliefs have consequences for our lives. It is important to understand that our beliefs are what motivate our behaviour. The attitudes about life we hold have a direct bearing on the way in which we behave. Recently I read again the verse in 1 Peter that says,

> *"Therefore, prepare your minds for action."* (1 Peter 1:13)

The Bible shows here, and in various other places, the direct correlation between what we think and what we do, and how our mindset governs our behaviour. Michael, the young man who wrote to me, is struggling to study at the moment because he says he cannot concentrate. He is afraid he's not going to be able to finish his course because his mind is full of negative thinking about himself and his sense of inadequacy. He is actually setting himself up for failure. He *will* fail unless he tackles his ungodly beliefs about himself and it will become a self-fulfilling prophecy. He must stop telling himself that because he has failed before he is going to fail again and hear what God is saying to him.

The author Brennan Manning thought of himself as worthless, inferior and inadequate. We have to address thoughts like these which do not line up with the truth of God's Word about us, otherwise they will cause us much emotional pain and will threaten to derail our spiritual lives.

We are incredibly motivated to meet our basic needs. The fact is, if we feel little sense of worth and significance we will go out and do something in order to find it. The problem is that we look for all kinds of ways to do it rather than looking to God. If we lack significance we might become success orientated or a perfectionist. We might become a person who self-promotes all the time, boasting continually and always putting ourselves in the centre of the picture. We might become a people pleaser. Or we might become a control freak who tries to control their environment or other people all the time in order to keep feelings of insecurity at bay.

I have to confess that I am a bit of a control freak. I am a list person and I don't like it if things don't go according to *my* plan. Take supermarket shopping as a small example. My husband, David, is what I call a "charismatic" shopper, but I'm a "1662" shopper. I make my list, stick to it and I don't buy anything extra. If you have the 1662 Prayer Book you know exactly where you are going in a church service and know what's coming next. If you are a bit more charismatic then often you have no idea what's coming next and you don't really mind. David takes that approach to shopping, but I like to be in control!

Each of us adopts behaviour that is designed to meet our needs or to dull the pain of not having them met. We may pursue alcohol, drugs, attention seeking, retail therapy, sex, food or any number of things. Some of these things are not bad in themselves, but we need to come to a place of realisation where we see that, in fact, only God can truly meet our needs. Jeremiah 2:13 says,

> "My people have committed two sins:
> They have forsaken me,
>   the spring of living water,

and have dug their own cisterns,
> *broken cisterns that cannot hold water."*

Here God says that people have a tendency to think they can meet their own needs, but in reality He is the only One who can truly satisfy us. When we try to meet our basic needs by ourselves we are going outside the will of God, trying to dig our own wells instead of asking Him for living water. In the end, God says, our methods will fail.

Same scenario, different reactions

If our beliefs affect our actions and the way we behave, equally they affect how we view events that happen to us in life. What we have come to believe about all manner of things – about ourselves, others, about people in authority, about sex and relationships, about God and our relationship with Him – all these provide the filter through which we process events that are happening to us now. Take the following scenario:

Two young men, both employed by the same business, are called into the boss's office on the same day and told they are being made redundant. They are given a package of redundancy pay and told they are free to go because there is no more work for them. They both experience exactly the same thing, but each young man reacts very differently.

Once man gets in his car and drives home at a rate of knots to his wife, so excited he hardly knows what to do with himself.

The other young man gets in his car and drives down to the beach. He pulls up on the front, looks at the water and thinks to himself, "I wish I could die." In a black cloud of depression he seriously contemplates suicide.

The activating event was exactly the same, so what is the difference?

The first young man was thinking, "This is my great opportunity! I've always wanted to start my own business, but I've never had the money to do it." Now he and his wife are delighted because this has given them a platform from which they can launch out and do their own thing.

The other young man is thinking, "I'm a failure. I've always been a failure and now everyone is going to know it. I can't face this any more." He feels worthless, inadequate and inferior. The consequences for him, therefore, are completely different.

This is how our assumptions and beliefs have a very real effect on our present circumstances. The second young man could also say, "Here is a golden opportunity for me to have a career change and start afresh." After all, he is still young and has lots of potential to his life. But his negative reaction belies a set of beliefs that indicate he probably comes from a background in which he was never affirmed or encouraged. He views this latest event as another in a long line of disasters where he has failed to live up to his parents' expectations.

Carrying these kinds of negative beliefs around with us can be debilitating. If we are frightened of failing, like the young man above, then we will spend most of our time working hard to please others. When we are faced with some challenge we will put pressure on ourselves by thinking, "I must get this right" because we are desperate to receive affirmation. The problem with this is it's like trying to fill a bucket with holes in it. We keep filling it with water and it just keeps leaking out. However much affirmation we receive, it is never adequate. What we really need is God's affirmation.

We have to weed out all the ungodly beliefs we hold, imposed on us by past events, and replace them with godly beliefs based on the truth of God's Word. Too often, when we seek healing we focus only on our symptoms i.e. we feel depressed, anxious, fearful, and want those symptoms to go away, but we ignore our underlying beliefs. Unless we address our fundamental beliefs, whatever ministry we receive will be ineffective and the symptoms will only return later.

That's why Paul tells us in Romans 12:2 that we need to renew our minds, and why, in Ephesians 4:22, he talks about "putting off" our old self which has been corrupted by deceitful desires and urges us to *"be made new in the attitude of your minds."* When our core beliefs change, then our behaviour will follow. We counter the lies we have come to believe by applying the truth, so we must constantly examine our thinking to see where it is going wrong.

Dallas Willard says, "Your system is perfectly arranged to get the results you are getting. If you don't like the results you're getting then you have to look at your system." In other words, we need to tackle our problems at the root – our thought processes – and work at pulling down and changing those "locked-in" patterns of thought and behaviour.

Three factors that affect our thinking

Aside from the beliefs that have become embedded in us during our formative years, three more factors compound the problem of our ungodly beliefs and thought processes. Each of these seeks to bend us to its way of thinking.

1. The world
The culture in which we live has a significant effect on our thinking. We live in a fallen world whose mindset is contrary to God and whose values are constantly shifting and changing to suit the public mood. In these days people continually question whether there can be any such thing as absolute truth. They say, "Your truth is as good as my truth. We can do what we like; we just need to be free to do our own thing, to be true to ourselves ..."

Recently I was absorbed by the television show *The Apprentice* with Sir Alan Sugar. In one episode, where there were three candidates left, all competing for a job with Sugar's organisation, Sugar was being really belligerent and was having a go at them when one girl decided to stick up for another girl. Immediately Sugar turned on her and said, "You can't do that! That won't get you the job. We don't want any pally stuff here. You need to look out for Number 1." As soon as I heard that I thought, "Oh, that's the world speaking, isn't it?" We have rights, we've got to speak up for ourselves, we have to be comfortable and satisfied. This is the kind of thinking the world wants to impose on us.

The world will tell us that we must be free to do our own thing, get whatever we want, use our body however we want to meet our needs for love and security our way. But we must not be taken in by the world and its norms. Henri Nouwen speaks about "unmasking the world around us" and this is very apt. We have to unmask the lies that the world constantly tries to feed us, otherwise those lies will motivate our actions and we will go off track.

2. The flesh

Because we are fallen creatures we have a natural bias away from God and towards sin. Our flesh is constantly intent on meeting its own needs. It is the Jeremiah scenario once again: we try to dig our own wells but we have broken cisterns that leak water.

Our flesh can be incredibly demanding. It cries out constantly for satisfaction – which is why we fall so often and go our own way instead of God's. As long as we live, the struggle between pleasing our flesh and obeying the Holy Spirit will always exist.

In another TV programme called *The Convent*[1] there was a young girl called Victoria who, on one occasion, talked openly about her relationships. She had a husband, but she also had another guy whom she loved. She said her husband knew about this other relationship and she claimed that the arrangement suited all three of them and that her husband was very happy about it because "he wants me to be true to myself". I thought, "What rubbish!" Who is she being true to? Only her fallen nature! Such an emotional tangle will only make her and these two men miserable in the end. There is no happy ending to that.

The fact is, our flesh will always lie to us about our needs and we must not be taken in by it. The needs of the flesh arise out of our own woundedness and we broadcast confused messages to ourselves. Our flesh will complain to us constantly saying, "This is what I need" but the only solution is to align ourselves with the truth of God's Word and look to Jesus to be the sole provider of our needs.

3. The devil

Each of these three enemies side with one another to influence our thinking. Our enemy Satan tends to ride in on the back of the world's skewed thinking and our fleshly desires to whisper in our ear and fan the flames of sinful desire. Our wrong beliefs are reinforced as the devil lies to us, telling us how our needs will be met if only we will follow the path he is suggesting.

I am not talking here about demonization, but the ordinary spiritual warfare that every Christian is involved in constantly. Our fallen nature gets up before we do every single morning and Satan is right there, fanning the flame!

Jesus had to deal with the subtle lies of the enemy just as we do. After an intense forty days of fasting in the wilderness the enemy came to tempt Him to misuse His power and authority. He said to Jesus, in effect, "You've got needs, meet those needs Your own way. If You want to be famous, do this." And wouldn't we all love to be famous? "You don't have to go to the cross," Satan suggested. "There is a quicker way. You can bypass the suffering and do it this way."

Jesus responded with the truth of God's Word to counter each temptation and we have to do the same. Jesus answered the enemy the same way each time: *"It is written . . . it is written . . . it is written."* He countered the lies with the truth. We have to learn how to unmask the enemy's lies and counter-attack with biblical truth. That is how we replace our old beliefs with new ones.

The good news for us is that our God speaks to us constantly and is only too willing to help us in our vulnerability. When we truly want to do business with Him, and acknowledge that we have beliefs that need changing because they are affecting our attitudes and behaviour, then He will come to our aid and help us to plug into kingdom thinking. In the next chapter we will look at a number of keys that will help us to break down the stronghold of ungodly beliefs and immerse ourselves in the truth.

Summary

Our beliefs motivate our behaviour. What we think leads to what we do. If we think of ourselves as worthless or inferior it can cause us great emotional pain. Because we are motivated to meet our basic human need for self-worth and affirmation, we might seek to do so in a number of unhelpful ways i.e. becoming people-pleasers or control freaks.

The same activating event will have completely different consequences for different people because of their differing beliefs about themselves and life. Carrying around negative beliefs will be debilitating and hold us back from progressing in our spiritual lives. Our ungodly beliefs need to be weeded out and replaced with godly beliefs based on the truth of God's Word.

Three main factors conspire to distort our thinking and reinforce those ungodly beliefs:

1. *The world.* Culture and society constantly feed us messages about pleasing ourselves, doing our own thing and getting what we want on our terms.
2. *Our flesh.* We are fallen creatures and have a natural bias away from God. Our flesh cries out for satisfaction and we face a constant battle between listening to the needs of our flesh or the direction of the Holy Spirit. We need to be aware that our flesh speaks out of its woundedness and align ourselves with God's truth.
3. *The devil.* The enemy uses both these factors to whisper lies to us about where and how our needs can be met. This is a normal part of spiritual warfare for the Christian.

Notes

1. In *The Convent* people were given the chance to spend forty days with a community of nuns. Each volunteer had deep-seated personal issues and was there to see if they could find the strength to change their lives back in the outside world.

CHAPTER

3

Steps Towards Freedom

Having identified that our beliefs are the source of our problems, what can we do about it? I believe there are a number of keys that will help us as we seek God's supernatural, sovereign healing in our lives and begin to move towards true freedom. In this chapter we will look at these solutions.

A hunger to be whole

First, a hunger to be whole is vital. No one changes without a hunger to be different. In order to take hold of the fullness of Christ's freedom there will be some hard work and discipline involved. Unless we are hungry for it we won't get there.

A couple of Christmasses ago I broke my arm and sprained my shoulder in the process. One of the main irritations of this for me was that I could no longer blowdry my hair by myself, so I made it my aim to at least get my shoulder healed as quickly as possible so that I could lift it above my head. I went to see a physiotherapist and then worked relentlessly at the exercises they gave me until I was mobile enough to do my hair for myself once again.

The funny thing was, once I was able to do that, I wasn't so keen to keep up the exercises any more. Once I had reached my goal I began to plateau. I realised then that if I was going to get myself back to full fitness I would have to carry on and do the necessary exercises and not give up. Similarly, unless we are committed to receiving God's healing in our lives, we won't do the work that is involved. That's why hunger is so important.

We have to take responsibility

Many people think that it is solely God's or perhaps their church's responsibility to get them healed, but actually a large part of the responsibility rests with us. Of course, in the Church we should be there to help and support one another, but in the end the responsibility for our healing is ours with God. Philippians 2:12–13 says,

> *"Continue to work out your salvation [sozo,* meaning "wholeness"] *with fear and trembling, for it is God who works in you to will and to act according to his good purpose."*

Wholeness comes by God working it in us and us working it out. In other words, we work at it together. Our task in the partnership is to make ourselves open and vulnerable before God and to bring that hurting, often hidden, part of ourselves to Him.

Some people have referred to this as the "child within". Some years ago I wrote a book about this called *Yesterday's Child* which speaks about the fact that we have the child of our past still living within us. The sum of everything that has happened to us in the past is still active inside us unless there has been some kind of resolution through healing. We have to take responsibility for that hurting part of ourselves by disclosing it to God and being willing to give Him access to it. Complete healing will not be possible until we do.

A friend of mine grew up with a mother who was always verbally abusive towards her and had a habit of saying, "You are so disgusting" to her every time she had an accident or did something wrong. Even if she did something quite trivial like spilling a glass of water her mother would say, "Oh, you are so disgusting." My friend grew up to be an extremely able lady with a high-flying profession, but inside she still thought of herself as "disgusting". When I was praying for her on one occasion she actually curled up into a foetal position and cried, "I'm so disgusting. Nobody would ever want to really know me. Nobody will ever really love me." Buried beneath the front of adequacy, ability and intelligence was a hidden child who still believed the lie that they were disgusting.

What this lady had done is what many people do with their bad feelings – try to squash them and deny their existence. She pushed her feelings down deep inside and said, "Go away! I don't like you. I don't want you. Get out of my life!" But all she was doing was burying her feelings alive. They would never go away until the hurt she suffered was resolved. For all of us the child we once were – the un-affirmed, criticised, maybe abused, put down or bullied child – is still there and will remain until it is healed. Try as we might we cannot stifle the cries of the child who is shouting to be healed.

A number of years ago I was receiving some ministry when it seemed that I had reached a plateau. Try as I might, I could not get any further on in my healing. After praying about it, however, I received a dream from God in which He showed me that I was responsible for bringing the child of my past to Him for healing.

In the dream I was getting ready for my own wedding. I was standing in front of a mirror, dressed all in white, and I was busy arranging my veil. Finally, when I was ready, I turned around to see if my bridesmaids were also ready. There was one gorgeous little bridesmaid with her posy, sitting on a step looking very demure and sweet. I looked at her and thought, "Ah, lovely." Then I looked around for the second bridesmaid, but I couldn't see her anywhere. I went to look for her outside and there, to my horror, was this little girl sitting on a step in Wellington boots and a pair of shorts with a grubby face. Her hair was all over the place and she had on a dirty shirt. "Goodness me!" I cried out. "Will somebody please do something? Will somebody come and get this bridesmaid ready? She needs cleaning up!" But nobody came. In the end I thought, "I'm going to have to do it. I'm going to have to get this child ready!" Then I woke up.

As I awoke I knew immediately that I had to take responsibility for that grubby child within me if I was going to get any further in my spiritual life. The yesterday's child that I kept pushing away needed to be healed. We would all love someone else to get that child cleaned up and healed for us, but we have to do it. Someone once said, "One of the mistakes many of us make is that we keep trying to have a better past. Life does not work that way. Your past is never going to improve, but your future can improve if you turn loose the past."[1]

A few years ago I saw a film about the life of Marie Balter called *Nobody's Child*.[2] At the age of seventeen Marie was suffering from severe depression and panic disorder. She was misdiagnosed as a schizophrenic and sent to Danvers State Mental Hospital, Michigan, where she was confined under that diagnosis for seventeen years. She would have terrible recurrent nightmares during which she would scream endlessly so that the hospital staff would lock her in a padded cell. But during her time there one staff member studied her behaviour and one day said to her, "Marie, you are going to be here for the rest of your life unless you do something about it. You should not be in here, this is not your place; you should be out there. But you are the one who is going to have to take responsibility for yourself and get yourself out."

Her recovery was very painful and gradual, but she was determined to take responsibility for her life. She began attending a therapy group in the hospital and after a lot of hard work she made enough progress to get herself out of there. Eventually her life turned around to the extent that she got her own apartment, got married, earned a degree in psychology and a Master's degree from Harvard in administration planning and public policy. Amazingly, she later returned in triumph as the administrator of Danvers State Mental Hospital, where she had spent all those years as a patient, and she became a nationally known advocate for those with mental health issues.

Before she reached a place of wholeness she continued to have terrible flashbacks. In these flashbacks she would see a picture of a tiny little girl who was locked in a cellar in the pitch black for hour after hour. Marie had been adopted as a child, but had been badly treated by her adoptive parents. The moment she had a flashback of herself as that little girl she would flip and literally run away from the horrible memory. The film of her life ends when Marie stands looking at herself in a mirror. She has one last flashback of her past and sees that streaky-faced, tormented child standing before her. She has the urge to scream and run as before, but this time she hesitates and reaches out her hands towards the child. You see her actually taking hold of the child in the film and the next shot is of Marie lying on her bed with this child in her arms. Then the child merges into her and they become one. That is her final moment of healing.

We have to take responsibility for that part of ourselves that needs healing and bring it to Jesus. God is on the side of the broken hearted and He can use many different ways to heal us, sometimes surprising ways. Brennan Manning's healing came one day when he was praying and God gave him a vision of his mother as a little girl. He saw her at six years of age in the orphanage where she grew up, with her nose pressed up against the window pane. She was looking out of the window, praying and asking God to send her two nice people to adopt her and she was crying. Manning said that as he saw that vision, all the anger he had towards his mother evaporated. In the vision he began to cry himself and was able to approach his mother and ask her to forgive him. With a radiant smile she said to him, "I may have messed up, but you turned out OK." Then she hugged him and kissed him in his vision. He commented that "... at that point the greatest enemy of trust was disarmed."

Whenever we experience healing, the element of forgiveness is almost always a part of the process. Marie Balter said that she would not have grown at all if she had not learned to forgive: "If you don't forgive your parents or your children or yourself, you never get beyond anger. Forgiving is the way of reaching out from a bad past and heading out to a more positive future."

Forgiveness is never easy or quick. It is something we work out. I often say to people, "Just tell God that you are willing to be made willing to forgive." Start on the first rung of the ladder and go from there. Keep working at it until eventually you are able to forgive those who have hurt you. It is the final resolution that will open the door to your healing.

We need to have kingdom goals

Something that will help us to stay on the road to freedom is making sure that the goals of our life are kingdom-focused and not short-term, self-satisfying goals. Sometimes we suffer from bad feelings and a sense of trapped-ness simply because we have set ungodly or unrealistic goals we think will fulfil our needs. Michael, the young man who wrote to me, said in his letter that he felt guilty and worthless. His logical answer to that was to pass his exams, which he thought would restore his self-worth. The reality is that was a short-term, transient goal that would not bring him lasting peace.

People have goals for all sorts of things: happiness, a better car, a job promotion, to be fit and healthy etc. All of these are good goals in themselves, but the Bible tells us in Proverbs 13:12, *"Hope deferred makes the heart sick."* In other words, when we set our heart on something and it doesn't happen we feel bad about it. So if we are suffering from difficult emotions we need to look to what unfulfilled goals may be causing them. Anger can always be traced to a blocked goal, anxiety to an uncertain goal and guilt to a failed or unreachable goal.

Michael feels depressed, guilty and anxious. He is depressed because he is beginning to think that his goal of being a person of worth is unreachable; guilty because he failed to pass his previous exam and now he's looking like he will fail his next one; anxious because his goal of feeling an OK person seems uncertain.

Many of our goals are not bad or sinful, they are just transient. They are self-satisfying goals, not kingdom goals. They belong to time and not eternity.

A number of years ago our son-in-law lost his job. At the time he and our daughter had two children and a third on the way, and for a while it looked as though they might have to come and live with us. I was really worried about the situation and I spiralled into anxiety. I began to pray like crazy every day, "O Lord, please find him another job. Lord, today may somebody offer him a job. May someone give them some money so they can get through the next week." I kept on praying like this, but the more I prayed the more anxious I became.

I continued in my anxiety because my hopes were uncertain and my prayers too earthbound. One day I realised what I was doing and changed my pattern of praying. I asked God to show me how to *"seek first the kingdom"* in my prayers. Up until then my goal had been happiness and security for them (so that I didn't have to worry about them, if the truth be told) but as kingdom people our goals have to be much bigger than that.

So, I began praying, "Lord, I pray that through this whole experience they will draw closer to You. I pray that they will experience Your goodness and mercy. I pray that they will learn lessons that You will build into the foundations of their lives . . . " As I began to do that I became very excited because in my heart I knew that God loved those prayers. Somehow I had hooked into kingdom thinking and immediately I felt my anxiety lift. Later our son-in-law got a fantastic job and they are now a lot better off than we are!

Meditating on the Word

Meditating on God's Word so that we constantly fill our minds with the truth is a wonderful way of silencing the onslaught of skewed thinking from the world, our flesh and the devil.

Jeremiah wrote, *"When your words came, I ate them; they were my joy and my heart's delight"* (Jeremiah 15:16). I love Jeremiah's directness and the way he describes "feeding" on God's words. Are we feeding on the Word in the way we should be? If we immerse ourselves in the truth then our defence is prepared when lies try to bend our thinking.

I believe many of us are too legalistic about our quiet times. We have our time with God each morning or evening and we are locked into one particular way of reading our Bibles. I'm not knocking that, because it's a good discipline, but we need to learn to meditate on the Word. Immediately, some will say, "Oh, I'm no good at that", but I would suggest that, in fact, most of us are absolutely brilliant at it. Whenever someone criticises us, what do we do? We go away and think about what they've said and turn it over and over in our minds. That's meditation!

To try it out, I suggest taking a passage of Scripture, Ephesians chapter 1 for instance, and read it substituting "I" for "we" and "me" for "us" to personalise it. Take just one verse of the passage per day and go over and over it. Think about it while you are driving to the supermarket, heading to work, having your lunch break, or whenever. Then take Psalm 139 and go over that one verse at a time. Make sure you limit yourself to a single verse and really work on it. Take a whole month to work through that one psalm if necessary until you find the Word of God goes deep down inside you and begins to work in you.

There are no rules to reading the Bible. We can take a whole year to read and meditate upon a single book if we want to, gradually imbibing it so that it is thoroughly implanted in our spirit. It's great to read the whole Bible and to see the overall scheme of things, but so much more important to have the truth of the Word buried deep inside us, written on our heart and hidden away where it can never be changed or eradicated.

Listen to God's voice

God can also speak to us in other ways apart from the Bible and we need to be alert and listening for the voice of the Holy Spirit in everyday life. We should expect God to speak to us through ordinary things, through friends, or through creation.

Once I was sitting in my lounge having just been reading a book called *Windows of the Soul* by Ken Gire – a fabulous book that I would recommend to anybody. I had just read a chapter where the author had been talking about hearing God by all sorts of means and I kept thinking to myself, "I must listen more to God." Then, as I swivelled my chair around and looked out of the window, my gaze rested on the house at the end of our garden. The house had scaffolding around it and it had been like that for several months. At first there had been lots of activity there, but then the work had stopped and the scaffolding had remained there for some time with no work going on. As I continued to look at it the Lord spoke to me and said, "Work in progress ... You are a work in progress." The words really hit me and I thought, "Wow, thank You,

Lord. I'm so glad I'm a work in progress. I haven't got there yet, but I am on a journey." Then God continued, "But the work can get held up. You can plateau." Then I thought, "Oh, I don't like that quite so much!"

Using the image of the house at the end of my garden, God drew my attention to the fact that I often plateau in my walk with Him. At times I coast along and am not really gripped by God. It made me realise that I needed to watch out and not be complacent, to keep pressing into God for more of Him.

God will speak to us in all sorts of ways, we just have to be alert and listening. Proverbs 8:34–35 says,

> *"Blessed is the man who listens to me,*
> *watching daily at my doors,*
> *waiting at my doorway.*
> *For whoever finds me finds life*
> *and receives favour from the* LORD.*"*

Recognition and repentance

Once we have recognised that our beliefs are having an adverse effect on our behaviour we have to act accordingly to correct them. Recognising how they were formed is half the battle, but then change has to come.

I remember the very first time I wrote a book. When I had completed the manuscript I handed David a copy of it to read. As he began to read the first few pages I watched as he took a pen out of his pocket and began marking corrections. Outraged, I literally snatched the manuscript our of his hands and said, "Well, that's it then isn't it? I'm hopeless. I'm not a writer." Shocked, he said, "What on earth is wrong with you?" "I'm useless!" I exclaimed, "I can see you writing all over it." David replied, "I'm just correcting some of the spelling and grammar here and there. Do you want my help or not?"

At that point I had to stop and think, to get things into perspective. "This man loves me," I told myself. "He is for me, he's on my side. I don't doubt that for one instant." I knew David loved me and wanted to help me and, therefore, he was not out to hurt or destroy me. That meant I could accept his criticism of my work, because he just wanted to help me improve on what I had done.

Whenever we recognise an ungodly belief at work in our lives the next step is repentance. There won't be any real change in our lives without it; it is a key step in the journey to freedom. Then after repentance change must come. We need to ask God to show us how to think differently, to behave differently from now on.

I was born the last child of four children in our family. I was something of a surprise to my parents, born when my mother was around forty years old, so there was quite an age gap between me and my siblings. My birth was sort of inconvenient for my parents, firstly because they thought they had completed their family and hadn't anticipated more children, and secondly because they ran a family business and having a baby around made things difficult. Now, I always knew that I was loved, there was no doubt in my head about that, but I always felt that I was a bit of an inconvenience, which I was actually!

My mother made light of it all. When we were out shopping and she bumped into someone she knew who commented, "Oh, I didn't know you had another little one!" my mother would always answer light-heartedly, "Oh, you know, our little 'mistake'!" and grin. In one sense it was quite nice to be the centre of attention, but on another level the idea that I was a "mistake" or an "accident" went in very deeply. It became a core belief that began to affect the way I behaved as I grew older.

The consequences of this were many and varied. One result was that I virtually needed a gold-lettered invitation to go anywhere. I didn't feel welcome at any social event unless I had been specifically invited and was expected. This feeling continued into adulthood and really caused me problems when later on I became a vicar's wife. Vicar's wives are meant to go and visit people to pray with them – that's what they do! I would think about a person at church and say to myself, "I must go and visit them", but I would get in the car, drive to their house, and then sit outside in the car unable to go in. Sometimes I even got as far as their front door and then turned around and went away without knocking. I always thought, "I'm not expected, it'll be inconvenient." I would drive back home and say to myself, "I'll do it another day," but another day would come and the same thing would happen.

Then, one day as I was reading Scripture, God spoke to me in such a way that He moved a verse I'd read many times from my head to my heart. It was in Colossians where it says we are chosen by God and dearly loved (Colossians 3:12). That word "chosen" hit me and suddenly, for the very first time, I recognised the fact that although I may have been a "mistake" in my mother's eyes, in all eternity I was "chosen" by God. So which one was I going to believe? That I was unplanned by my parents was true, but it was only a tiny fragment of the real truth. The bigger truth that really counted *was* that I was planned and chosen by Almighty God from the foundation of the world. He had planned and purposed for me to be born.

Every morning when I wake up I have a choice: which truth will I choose to align myself with? Every day I decide to go God's way and to believe His truth. Of course, I have my bad days, we all do, but the more we do the right thing – i.e. the more we choose to walk in our chosenness – the more we are able to push through those bad feelings and the easier it becomes to walk in the truth of Christ. Choosing to apply biblical truth to our minds has to become a habit. This positive habit will break our old, bad habits as the truth of the Word is embedded in our heart.

Summary

Having identified our beliefs as the root of our problems and lack of emotional freedom, various factors will help us to move forward:

1. *A hunger to be whole.* No lasting change will occur in our lives unless we are fully committed to travelling the road to freedom.

2. *Taking responsibility.* God desires to heal us, but we are responsible for opening up to Him, making ourselves vulnerable and bringing the hurting "yesterday's child" to Him for healing. We also need to be open to the many ways in which God might heal us and not try to box Him in.

3. *Having kingdom goals.* Our thinking and our prayers need to be directed towards God's kingdom agenda for our lives, rather than being short-term, transient and self-seeking.

4. *Meditating on the Word.* Constantly filling our mind with God's truth will silence the multiplicity of ungodly thoughts.

5. *Listening for God's voice in other ways.* God can speak to us through everyday life situations so we need to be alert to hear Him.

6. *Recognition and repentance.* We need to recognise where our skewed beliefs are adversely affecting our behaviour and reverse the trend beginning with repentance.

Every day we face a choice: to go along with our ungodly beliefs or to go God's way and believe the truth of His Word about us.

Notes

1. Quote attributed to Rev. Thomas Lane Butts in his article "On Winning the Biggest Battle of Life".

2. Also a book by Marie Balter and Richard Katz, *Nobody's Child*, Addison Wesley Publishing Co., 1992. ISBN 978–0201608168.

Developing the Key of Trust

Ruthless trust

Changing our beliefs in order to change our behaviour is vital if we want to be free, but one thing that will help us move forward on our journey more than anything else is learning to really trust God.

This is something that has really sunk into my spirit over the last couple of years. Of course, we all know that as Christians we are supposed to trust in God. That's fairly obvious. But I have begun to see in a new way just how pivotal trust is on our path to freedom. It started for me when I read Brennan Manning's book *Ruthless Trust* and realised that trust is the one thing in life we absolutely cannot do without. Trust enables us to take risks with new thinking and new behaviour. It gives us the courage to become the new creation that Jesus says we are. Proverbs 3:5 says,

> *"Trust in the LORD with all your heart*
> *and lean not on your own understanding;*
> *in all your ways acknowledge him,*
> *and he will make your paths straight."*

Trust will change us. Trusting God so that we take Him at His word means we can live out of our new identity in Christ; to live as a chosen person instead of a mistake or an accident. It gives us the courage to walk as a loved person instead of a rejected one; to be a "somebody" in God's eyes instead of the nobody we've always felt like.

Trust will enable us to behave differently towards others; to express our need of them when we have been used to living independently; to trust people when we had decided never to do it again; to love others instead of always keeping them at arm's length because we are terrified of being let down again; to be spontaneous when we have been used to being a control freak.

I have been on my own journey with being a control freak. As I've already mentioned I am very much a list person who likes to plan out my day and stick to my agenda. I don't tend to be very spontaneous. It makes me feel good to have my list for the day ahead and know exactly what I'm doing at 11.00 am, what I'll be doing at 2.00 pm, and so on. I suppose it makes me feel secure. Recently, as I was busy at home, the telephone rang and it was Debbie, my daughter. She said, "Mum, we haven't seen you for ages. We're on our day off – why don't you and Dad just get in the car and come and see us?" Because I had my agenda for the day I said, "No, we can't possibly do that, darling, we're far too busy." But David came into the room and asked what was going on and when I told him he said, "Well, let's go then." "But we've got lots to do," I protested. "Nothing that can't wait," he replied.

He was right, of course. I had my diary with some little ideas about what I was going to do but, yes, those things could wait. I had a choice: to be spontaneous and go with the flow or to control my environment, control David, and stick rigidly to my plan. I'm glad to say I went with it. We visited Debbie and her family and we had such a fun time. We spent the night there and the next day with them and had a great time together. I'm so glad that God is beginning to free me up in this area because you miss out on so much when you're a control freak.

Trust also enables us to let our mask down to others, to allow them to see that bit of vulnerability that exists inside us and just be real for a change. Brennan Manning writes this in the preface to *Ruthless Trust*:

> "During the past three years of prayer, study and soul searching the Holy Spirit has guided me to an inescapable conclusion: ruthless trust is the way for this ragamuffin. If it be your way, the sign you can trust will be the slow, steady miraculous transformation from self-rejection to self-acceptance, rooted in the acceptance of Jesus Christ."

Trust is a risky business, which is why I like Manning's title, "ruthless trust". Trusting in the God that you cannot see, who you can't always hear very clearly, hanging in there by your fingernails at times, takes courage and guts. The Bible instructs us to *"trust in the* LORD *... and lean not on [our] own understanding"*. The fact is, we would rather have *"understanding"* than trust most of the time. Throughout I am endeavouring to help us gain some understanding about where our problems come from, but I will say again that having an understanding of it will not heal us. Trust, however, will begin the healing process and see it through to completion.

In his book Manning tells the story of the ethicist John Cavanagh. Cavanagh was searching for direction in his life and decided that he needed to go and visit Mother Teresa in Calcutta. When he arrived there, Mother Teresa asked him if there was something she could do for him. He told her, "Mother, pray that I have clarity." She looked him straight in the eye and said, "No, I won't do that." Surprised, Cavanagh asked why not. Mother Teresa replied, "Because clarity is the last thing you are clinging to and you must let go of it." When Cavanagh commented that she always seemed to have clarity about the direction her life should take she answered saying,

"No, I've never had clarity. What I have always had is trust. So I pray that you will have trust."

Manning adds that by craving clarity we try to eliminate the risk of trusting God. We always like to know where we are heading, to understand situations and to have reasons for the things that happen to us, but walking with God is not generally like that. We have lots of questions about life that we would like answering, such as the big questions regarding suffering and we can search for the answers to those things, but in the end no answer will satisfy us. What will satisfy us is trusting in God, knowing that He knows best, that He is a good God and knows what He is doing. When things go wrong and everything looks bad we can say to ourselves, "This is happening, but God is good and His love endures forever. I will trust in the goodness and mercy of God, even though I don't understand what is happening to me." Nothing delights the heart of God more than when we don't understand, but choose to trust Him anyway.

A woman called Henrietta Mears, born in the 1900s in America, was partially sighted, almost blind, but nevertheless developed a huge ministry to children that spread all over the United States. She believed that God had called her to train the next generation of leaders for the Church and she lived with immense courage and faith. Among the thousands of young people she impacted, Billy Graham was one, and he often said, "My mother, my wife and Henrietta Mears are the three women who have most impacted my life." Towards the end of her life Henrietta was asked if there was anything she would have done differently and she said, "I wish I had trusted Christ for more. I wish I had prayed riskier prayers. I wish I had asked for bigger mountains. I wish I had taken scarier risks."

We don't want to get to the end of our lives and wish we had trusted Jesus for more – to know that He could have healed us more, resolved the issues in our life, sorted out the rubbish, if only we had trusted Him a little bit more. So what are we going to do? We need to do some spiritual spring cleaning and let go of some things and we need to cultivate trust. You may say, "I've tried to trust God more, I really have, but I can't do it." If that is you, I offer the following tips to help you develop the amazing key of trust.

1. Focusing on the bigness of God

First of all it is helpful to focus on what God is like and think about His character. God is immense. The Bible says He is the creator of all things. He is beyond our imaginings, infinitely glorious, wonderfully powerful and amazingly loving. I think we are so used to praying to our Father that we have somehow shrunk Him, reducing Him down to our size. If we recapture our wonder of God we will find it easier to trust Him.

Remember the wonderful story where Jesus, who is hungry and exhausted after a day's ministry, gets into a boat with His disciples and they set off for the other shore? We read that,

> "He got into the boat and his disciples followed him. Without warning, a furious storm came up on the lake, so that the waves swept over the boat. But Jesus was sleeping. The disciples went and woke him, saying, 'Lord, save us! We're going to drown!' "
>
> (Matthew 8:23–25)

The question I have is, why were the disciples panicking so much when they had the Creator of the Universe in the boat with them? The answer is because they took Him as they saw Him: a man who was their shape and size. This is what we do to God all the time. We shrink Him so that in our eyes He no longer looks like the amazing God of all creation.

In 1994 my husband, David, was in Toronto at the Airport Christian Fellowship. He was there to take some time out just to soak in God's presence. At one meeting he attended, while he was just enjoying the Lord's presence lying on the floor, a guy at the very back of the hall began shouting at the top of his voice, "BIG GOD . . . BIG GOD!" David thought, "Well, he'll stop in a minute", but he didn't. He went on continually shouting "BIG GOD!" David became more and more irritated by this and began thinking, "Why doesn't somebody tell that fellow to shut up? At least he could shout something more theologically correct like 'Almighty God!' " But then he felt the Holy Spirit nudge him and say, "David, listen . . . listen to what he is saying." Suddenly David thought to himself, "He's right. God is a BIG, BIG GOD!" We are so used to that phrase "Almighty God" that we can miss the bigness of it.

"Big God" is a very apt description. He is "big" beyond our wildest dreams. And yet, God still knows our thoughts and concerns Himself with us. Psalm 139:1–4 tells us,

> *"O LORD, you have searched me*
> *and you know me.*
> *You know when I sit and when I rise;*
> *you perceive my thoughts from afar.*
> *You discern my going out and my lying down;*
> *you are familiar with all my ways.*
> *Before a word is on my tongue*
> *you know it completely, O LORD."*

God knows us so intimately that He even knows everything we are about to say. Later in verse 18 of this psalm we read that God's thoughts are more numerous than the grains of the sand. If I were to wet my finger and put it into a little bit of sand, then attempt to count those grains, there would be hundreds and hundreds of them just in that tiny sample. Now imagine how many billions and trillions of grains there must be in the Sahara desert. God's thoughts are bigger and more numerous than all of those grains. This is the vastness of God's mind.

We often quote the verse in Isaiah which says, *" 'For my thoughts are not your thoughts, neither are your ways my ways,' declares the* LORD*"* (Isaiah 55:8). I think we sometimes quote that glibly. We think that God's thoughts and ways are "a bit different" from ours, but no, they are radically different! So different that we will never fathom them as long as we live.

God is a Creator God and He created our universe. Just think about that for a moment. There are possibly 125 billion galaxies in the Universe. The Milky Way is one of the smaller galaxies, and yet it is estimated to contain between 200 and 400 billion stars. God created all of that. Think about that and then listen to the words of Psalm 147. Verse 3 shows how intimately God cares for us:

"He heals the brokenhearted
and binds up their wounds."

Then the psalmist says in the same breath,

"He determines the number of the stars
and calls them each by name." (verse 4)

Add up 125 billion galaxies and multiply that by 400 billion stars and think about the fact that God knows each of those stars by name! And at the same time He knows all our thoughts and can heal our broken heart. This is awesome stuff! We need continually to remind ourselves of the "otherness" of God. God is our Abba Father and Jesus is our friend, but He is also the awesome Creator. Focusing on this will help us to trust in this amazing God, that He knows what is best for us and will guide our life.

2. Intimacy
Intimacy leads to courageous trust. Intimacy with God is like a rich soil that helps to cultivate the plant of trust. Men of faith

like Moses, David and Paul trusted God because they knew Him intimately.

The more I get to know my friends or my husband, the more I trust them. That doesn't mean to say they do everything the way I like it, because they don't. David, for instance, is very untidy, even though every year I hope there might be a little improvement! But I do trust him. I trust him and I trust my friends, because I have been intimate with them over many years. I have one friend who lives in South America who I have known since I was in my thirties. Because we've known each other for ages we talk for hours on the phone and email each other regularly. I totally trust her because I have known her intimately. I know that neither she nor any of my friends would do anything intentionally to harm me. Intimacy fosters trust.

In her book, *Always Enough*, Heidi Baker speaks about the transforming power of intimacy with Jesus. She writes,

> "Let Him love you. It is so much simpler than we thought. It is time to be transformed by His love, so that there is no fear in you. Perfect love casts out fear. Be wrecked for everything but His presence. Be so utterly abandoned to His love … God in His glory will pour His presence into people to the degree that entire nations will be transformed. He will pour His love out like a river, like an ocean … It is intimacy that transforms our lives. Nothing can replace it. No formulas, no systems, nothing can take the place of intimacy with our God."

And Brennan Manning writes this:

> "The recovery of passion starts with reappraising the value of the treasure, continues with letting the great Rabbi hold us against His heart, and comes to fruition in a personal transformation of which we will not even be aware."

When we get intimate with God, when we let this great Creator "hold us against His heart", something inside of us quietens and we are transported to a place where healing can flow to every part of our beings. It is during those times of intimacy that our souls are comforted and love begins to settle us.

How do we create intimacy with Jesus? I'm sure you know as well as I do that we need to set aside time. Time is something that seems in very short supply these days, but it is so important that we take time to just be with God. I mentioned earlier about the time when I broke my arm. Surprisingly, this accident was a real gift to me. It's not a lot of fun falling off a chair and breaking your arm while you're putting up Christmas decorations, but once it had happened I came to realise that I had more or less a month in front of me where I would be able to do very little, and I suddenly thought, "Thank You, Lord, you've given me a gift of time!" I used that time to pursue intimacy with Him and it was fantastic.

We don't have to get legalistic about spending time with God. Instead of trying to plan our time with Him religiously, we can make a decision to pursue God all the time and use any and every spare moment that comes to hand. We can steal a few moments with God in the car on the way to the supermarket, go for a walk and a chat with Him in our lunch break. We just need to form a habit of intimacy with Him.

When David and I were first married we grabbed every moment we could together amidst a busy church life and ministry. David would rush home from visiting someone just to spend a few minutes with me and kiss me before he dashed out again. We stole every moment we could to be with one another. We have to get like that with God. I'm not throwing discipline out of the window and saying planned times don't work, but we also need to be spontaneous.

Intimacy with us is what God wants above anything. He loves our service, when we minister to others, when we feed the poor, when we witness to our neighbours, but before our service He wants our intimacy. The primary call on our lives is to be intimate with God, to enter into that relationship where we are blessed by Him in order that we can go and be the blessing He intends to others.

That was the essence of God's covenant with Abraham: come in to be blessed and go out to be a blessing. Not "go out and bless people", but go and *be* a blessing. It's to do with *being* and not *doing*. We are a blessing because of who we are in Christ. Just by being ourselves we are a blessing to others because we have been blessed in the place of intimacy.

We need some ingenuity and imagination to take time out with God and we need some tenacity too. We can't have a couple of goes at spending time alone with God and then give up because we feel as though He didn't turn up. We have to hang in there and pursue Him with tenacity, then we will certainly find Him. When we seek and ask we will receive just as Jesus promised, but we need to develop some spiritual perseverance.

Intimacy grows out of commitment. Time, ingenuity, tenacity, none of these things will happen without it. So often we dip in and dip out of our relationship with Jesus. We heat things up after a conference or some other event, but then we cool off again. I found the following quote from Ken Gire shocking but true:

> "Jesus is not indiscriminately intimate. Often we want intimate disclosure without being serious about the relationship. If you think about it, that's not much different than having casual sex – wanting the pleasure of intimacy without commitment."

3. Gratitude

Lastly, trust grows out of gratitude. Thanksgiving and praise are powerful tools in our lives. Paul instructed the Philippians to pray about everything and to use thanksgiving in their prayers:

> *"Do not be anxious about anything, but in everything, by prayer and petition, with thanksgiving, present your requests to God. And the peace of God, which transcends all understanding, will guard your hearts and your minds in Christ Jesus."*
>
> (Philippians 4:6–7)

When we continually give God thanks and are committed to gratitude in our prayers, something happens inside of us. A change takes place. God's peace, which is far more wonderful than the human mind can understand, begins to fill us and alter our perspective.

Some time ago I read a lovely book called *Tuesdays with Morrie*[1] about a student's love for his mentor. Mitch is the former student and his old college professor and mentor, Morrie, is dying from motor neurone disease. Mitch decides to visit Morrie every Tuesday to spend time talking with him. One day Mitch asks Morrie if he ever feels sorry for himself. Morrie answers, "Well, sometimes in the morning, that's when I mourn. I feel around my body, move my fingers and my hand, whatever I can still move, and I mourn what I have lost. I mourn the slow, insidious way in which I'm dying. But then I stop mourning." "Just like that?" asks Mitch. "Well, I give myself a good cry if I need it, but then I concentrate on all the good things still in my life; on the people who are coming to see me, on the stories I'm going to hear, on you when it's Tuesday, because we are Tuesday people."

Morrie was real about his suffering, but he moved on from that and realised there was still much he could be grateful for.

Elizabeth Elliot, the missionary, came to our church many years ago to speak to a group of women. I remember one thing she said very clearly: "If only wives would concentrate on the 70% their husbands are, and not on the 30% they are not." (The same is true for husbands, of course.) Her words really hit me and I thought, "That is so true. I moan and groan at David and I keep nagging him to do this or that. Why don't I just think for a change about how wonderful he is, what a great father he has been, how he has always stuck up for me, how he has always been there for me, and how he always encourages me to try new things?" I can tell you, it really worked! But we have to make a choice to be thankful. Gratitude takes determination. It doesn't mean we have to be unreal, but it does take effort.

Gratitude also takes practise. It's easy to become anxious when you have a large family with twelve grandchildren, because there is always something going on with one of them. I have a tendency to go over things in my mind and worry about them, particularly when I get into bed at night. I may have already prayed about a situation and given it over to God, but as soon as I put my head on the pillow back it all comes and I'm going over it all again. To counteract the worry I use the following method: I start to praise God for all the good things He has done, say in a particular child's life, for all the gifting that child has been given, for all the ways in which good things have happened in their life. Or I just begin praising God for all the good things that have happened in my life and in our family, how God has blessed us in so many ways, and before I know it I'm asleep. The peace of God settles me because of that gratitude.

Gratitude is highly contagious and very attractive. We have a Nigerian family living a few doors away from us and recently they had a house warming and birthday party which we were invited to attend. I had never seen anything like it – people came in all their finery. There was colour everywhere! And before we ate, the Mama from Nigeria, who had flown in for this party, got up to give thanks to God. She led us all in singing first and then she prayed. For half an hour she gave thanks, nothing else, just gave thanks. She started off by saying, "I give You thanks, God, that my daughter is alive and not dead. I give You thanks that she is here in this place and is not sick in hospital. Thank You that she has children and is not barren, that she has a house and is not homeless . . . " She went on and on pouring out her thanks to God and it was wonderful and amazing to hear. Gratitude is the stuff of the kingdom.

Childlike trust

I read this story some time ago and it impacted me deeply. It reminded me how simple trusting in God can and should be, demonstrated through the faith of a child. This is the testimony of a Christian doctor working in Africa.

"One night we had worked hard to help a mother in the labour ward, but in spite of all we could do she died leaving us with a tiny premature baby and her crying two-year-old daughter. We would have difficulty keeping the baby alive as we had no electricity to run an incubator. We also had no special feeding facilities. Although we lived on the Equator, nights were often chilly with treacherous drafts.

One student midwife went for the box we had for such babies and the cotton wool that the baby would be wrapped in. Another went to stoke up the fire and fill a hot water bottle. She came back shortly, distressed, to tell me that in filling the bottle it had burst. Rubber perishes easily in tropical climates. 'And it was our last hot water bottle,' she exclaimed. As in the West it is no good crying over spilt milk, so in Central Africa it is no good crying over burst hot water bottles. They do not grow on trees and there are no drug stores down the forest pathways. 'Alright,' I said, 'put the baby as near to the fire as you safely can and sleep between the baby and the door to keep it free from drafts. Your job is to keep the baby warm.'

The following noon, as I did most days, I went to have prayers with any of the orphanage children who chose to gather with me. I gave the youngsters various suggestions of things to pray about and told them about the tiny baby. I explained about our problem of keeping the baby warm enough, mentioning the hot water bottle and that the baby could so easily die if it got chills. I also told them about the two-year-old sister crying because her mother had died. During the prayer time one ten-year-old girl, Ruth, prayed with the usual blunt conciseness of our African children, 'Please God, send us a water bottle. It'll be no good tomorrow, God, as the baby will be dead. So please send it this afternoon.'

While I gasped inwardly at the audacity of the prayer, she added, 'And while You're about it would You please send a dolly for the little girl so she'll know You really love her?' As often with children's prayers, I was put on the spot. Could I honestly say, 'Amen'? I just did not believe that God could do this. Oh yes, I know He can do everything, the Bible says so, but there are limits, aren't there?

The only way God could answer this particular prayer would be by sending me a parcel from my homeland. I had been in Africa for almost four years at that time and I had never ever received a parcel from home. Anyway, if anyone did send me a parcel, who would put in a hot water bottle? I lived on the Equator!

Half way through the afternoon while I was teaching in the nurse's training school, a message was sent that there was a car at my front door. By the time I reached home the car had gone, but there on the veranda was a large 22lb parcel. I felt tears pricking my eyes. I could not open the parcel alone, so I sent for the orphanage children. Together we pulled off the string, carefully undoing each knot. We folded the paper, taking care not to tear it unduly. Excitement was mounting. Some 30 or 40 pairs of eyes were focused on the large cardboard box. From the top I lifted out brightly coloured knitted jerseys. Eyes sparkled as I gave them out. Then there were the knitted bandages for the leprosy patients and the children looked a little bored. Then came a box of mixed raisins and sultanas. That would make a batch of buns for the weekend. Then, as I put my hand in again, I felt the . . . could it really be? I grasped it and pulled it out. Yes, a brand new rubber hot water bottle.

I cried. I had not asked God to send it. I had not truly believed that He could. Ruth was in the front row of the children. She rushed forward, crying out, 'If God has sent the bottle, He must have sent the dolly too!' Rummaging down to the bottom of the box she pulled out the small, beautifully dressed dolly. Her eyes shone. She had never doubted. Looking up at me she asked, 'Can I go over with you and give this dolly to that little girl, so that she'll know that Jesus really loves her?'

That parcel had been on the way for five whole months, packed up by my former Sunday school class whose leader had heard and obeyed God's prompting to send a hot water bottle even to the Equator, and one of the girls had put in a dolly for an African child five months before in answer to the believing prayer of a ten-year-old child, to bring it that afternoon. Before they call, I will answer."

Trust is the childlike dependence that God is looking for. Trust is life-changing. Trust means that we will walk in the truth regardless of how we feel because God has spoken. Trust means that we will walk in our chosenness because God has told us "You are chosen." We will change because we trust that what God says is true, not what the world, the flesh, the devil, or our past says to us.

We need to get healed from the hurts of the past, change the wrong beliefs that have produced ungodly habits in us and put into practice the amazing gift of trust. Pray for it, ask for it, call out for it, because you need it. We all need to be like little children and put our hand into the hand of our Father and simply walk with Him.

Summary

Changing our beliefs in order to change our behaviour is vital if we want to be free. One thing that will help us achieve that more than any other factor is the key of trust. Trust will enable us to take God at His word and it will also allow us to risk trying out new behaviour based on godly beliefs.

The following will help us develop the key of trust:

1. *Focusing on the bigness of God helps us to trust Him more.* We can trust God because, despite His vastness and His awesome power, He is intimately acquainted with our life, our problems and our needs.

2. *Intimacy leads to courageous trust.* The more we trust God the more we will be transformed by Him.

3. *Trust grows out of gratitude.* Thanksgiving and praise are powerful tools we can use to combat fear, anxiety, depression and other negative emotions.

Ruthless trust is childlike trust and this is the kind of dependence upon Him God is looking for.

Notes

1. Mitch Albom, *Tuesdays with Morrie: An Old Man, a Young Man, and Life's Greatest Lesson*, Time Warner, new ed. 2003.

CHAPTER

5

Letting Go of Regret

I wonder how much freedom you enjoy to worship God, unhindered by issues that would otherwise cloud your relationship with Him? How much freedom from worry do you have? From anxiety or fear? How much freedom to be the person God has called you to be and to be transformed into the image of Jesus? True freedom can seem an elusive thing. It is that most important key of trust that will release us if we can extend it into every area of our lives. But that is easier said than done. Trusting God involves us letting go – letting go and handing our lives over to Him.

As Christians we understand that our freedom had a cost attached to it which Jesus paid for. He paid that price on the cross to redeem our twisted lives, to restore our brokenness, to set us free from sin, fear and shame. That is a done deal. There is no cost to us for Christ's great sacrifice; if we put our faith in Jesus then that freedom is ours. The Bible says, *"If the Son sets you free, you will be free indeed"* (John 8:36). But we have to learn to walk in this freedom, to appropriate it for ourselves, to pick it up and use it, and this is where some of our difficulties arise – actually walking in that which Jesus has purchased for us. We find, like the young church leader, that there is some "cost" attached to God's freedom – the cost of letting go of the things that hold us back in order to fully receive and experience His freedom.

When it comes to fully surrendering ourselves to Jesus, many of us are like the rich young ruler who came to Him with a question about eternal life. I want us to look at this young man over the next couple of chapters because his story teaches us so much about "letting go" in order to truly gain our freedom.

The rich young ruler

The story of this young man's encounter with Jesus is brief, but significant, because it is mentioned in all of the Gospels except for John. In Mark he is referred to as a "rich young man", in Luke a "rich ruler", and in Matthew a "rich young ruler". Whenever I ask my husband, David, what I should preach about he will often say, "Speak on the rich young ruler. You've got three points right there: he's rich, he's young and he's a ruler!"

This young man comes to Jesus and asks Him a question: *"Good teacher ... what must I do to inherit eternal life?"* (Mark 10:17). Jesus answers him, *"You know the commandments: 'Do not murder, do not commit adultery, do not steal, do not give false testimony, do not defraud, honour your father and mother' "*, and the young man tells Jesus, *"All these I have kept since I was a boy."* Then there is a wonderful verse which tells us that Jesus looked at the man and loved him, then He said to him, *" 'One thing you lack ... Go, sell everything you have and give to the poor, and you will have treasure in heaven. Then come, follow me.' At this the man's face fell. He went away sad, because he had great wealth"* (Mark 10:21–22).

We read that the young man is very disappointed with the answer Jesus gives him. He hangs his head and walks away because he is extremely wealthy. Jesus then looks around at all His disciples and comments, *"How hard it is for the rich to enter the kingdom of God!"* (v. 23).

At this point Mark writes that the disciples were amazed

at these words and Jesus repeats, *"Children, how hard it is to enter the kingdom of God! It is easier for a camel to go through the eye of a needle than for a rich man to enter the kingdom of God"* (v. 24). Jesus' strange explanation seems puzzling to us at first. Some Bible commentators have taken His comments literally and say that His words denote impossibility because it is quite impossible for a camel to fit through the eye of a needle. Of course it is, but Jesus doesn't say it is "impossible" for a rich person to enter the kingdom of God, just *hard*. So what exactly does He mean?

At the time when Jesus was speaking all walled cities had gates. At the very least there would be a north and a south gate, if not a gate at each compass point. During the day these large gates were kept open as people entered and left the city, conducting their business. But as soon as dusk came the gates of the city were closed for security purposes. If you arrived at any city after dusk there was only one option: you had to enter through a very small gate that was set into the larger gates. It was such a squeeze that locals commonly referred to it as the "eye of the needle".

Imagine then a merchant trader arriving late at the city after a long, tiring day travelling across the hot, dusty terrain. His camel is weighed down with baggage – the rugs and spices he intends to sell in the city the following day. But the gates are locked and now he has a problem. How is he going to get his camel, his goods and himself into the city and find accommodation for the night? The answer is: not easily! He has to unload his camel and shove and push the beast through the small opening, leaving all his baggage outside, because there is no way can he get the camel and the baggage through at the same time.

Similarly, the rich young ruler was carrying a lot of baggage that came with his wealth. Jesus recognised it immediately and knew that it would hinder his spiritual pilgrimage. The young man would not progress any further unless he first laid aside the great weight that was holding him back.

For the young man his wealth was his baggage. The fact is, we each carry lots of baggage although what holds each of us back will be different. In order to enjoy the freedom of the kingdom we have to let a lot of things go.

As we walk the road to maturity in Christ challenges will come our way and sometimes we will pick up burdens which we then try to carry ourselves. We need to learn to release these burdens to God. If we try to carry them ourselves they will become like that "ball and chain", holding us back, weighing us down, or we will become like a merchant who refuses to unload his camel to get into the city and instead tries in vain to force his camel through the tiny gate.

Hebrews 12:1 instructs us to, *"throw off everything that hinders and the sin that so easily entangles, and run with perseverance the race marked out for us"*. We simply cannot run with perseverance if we are dragging a ball and chain behind us. Throughout our Christian lives, in order to enjoy the freedom of the kingdom, we have to learn how to unburden ourselves before God and this will mean different challenges for different people at different stages of their journey. The things that weigh us down – regrets, pain, hurt, anxiety, anger, frustration – all take our energy and attention; they fill our minds and prevent us from leading kingdom lives.

But particularly debilitating are what I call the "if onlys" and the "what ifs". The author Barbara Johnson said, "We crucify ourselves between two thieves: regret for yesterday and fear of what tomorrow might bring. These thieves steal our peace and joy."

The "If Onlys"

The "if onlys" of life are yesterday's regrets, those things we wished we had not done and those things we wished we had done. Bad choices and missed opportunities, something damaging we said to someone we love, a broken relationship, a child we didn't handle properly – there may be a hundred things we have regrets about. Unless they are handed over to Jesus and dealt with they can cause us shame, low self-esteem and even self-hatred.

A number of years ago my husband, David, attended a conference in America where he witnessed the unfolding drama of God dealing with one lady's "if only". At the meeting the speaker, well known for his prophetic ministry, singled out a lady in the crowd. He pointed at her and asked, "Is your name Margaret?" The woman nodded and so he asked her to stand up. Then he addressed the man sitting next to her who was her husband, "And are you John?" he asked. The man said that he was.

The minister asked them to confirm for the benefit of the congregation that he didn't know the couple and that they did not know him. Then he said to the woman, "Margaret, I have a message from God for you. He says to you, 'Margaret, it's all over. It's all over.'" He added something about a little boy being in the arms of Jesus and at that point she burst into tears and began to sob.

After the meeting David went over to speak with some people who had been sitting close to this lady and heard the full story. Eighteen months previously they had been working as missionaries in Africa. John announced that he was going to have a day off and go shooting with a couple of friends. They had two young sons and Margaret told him, "Oh, you must take the boys with you. You don't spend enough time with them." John protested and didn't want to take the boys, but his wife persisted and eventually she won. So John went off with the two boys and the most tragic accident occurred. During the course of the day the older boy accidentally shot the younger boy and killed him.

When they returned home their older son was devastated

and John was heartbroken. Margaret was caught up in a downward spiral of regret and told herself over and over again, "I forced them to go. I forced John to take the boys with him. If only I hadn't insisted on having my way."

The family returned home on an extended furlough and tried to recover from the incident. They spent a whole year working through their grief. At the end of that time John and their eldest son felt that it was time to go back and continue the work they had begun, but Margaret didn't want to. Months and months more went by and all she could say to John was, "I can't go back. It's not over, it's not over..."

It was at this point that some friends suggested they attend the conference that David was at. John and Margaret drove there, but even as they sat outside in the parking lot she had second thoughts about going into the meeting. She sat in the car and said she couldn't go in until, in despair, John said to her, "Margaret, it's over. It's over!"

It is normal to feel pain and loss. It's normal to grieve over things that have happened to us in the past. We have to work through those things. But of course there comes a time for all of us when we have to let them go and move on.

Once, when I was ministering in Europe, I met a young couple who asked me to pray with them. They were in their mid-thirties and had three lovely children, but they told me that they weren't involved in church life in any way and didn't feel able to be because they felt totally disqualified. They had met one another at university and begun dating. Everything was fine until one night they slept together and the girl found she was pregnant. They took the difficult decision that she should have an abortion because they felt they needed to finish their studies and couldn't cope with a baby. From then on they both carried a great deal of shame and regret and here they were, fifteen years on, still feeling excluded from any kind of ministry in church because of the weight of condemnation and remorse.

The mistakes of the past can cause us great sadness and

disappointment, because we regret falling short of God's standards, our own standards, or the hopes and expectations of others.

When David and I were missionaries in Chile I suffered from what I call a poverty mindset. Many missionaries survive on very little income and depend upon the support of others and it is easy to get into a mindset that says, "This is my lot in life, this is how it will always be." Back in the 1970s when I came home on furlough I was amazed, for instance, that everyone's houses were carpeted all the way through. I was used to seeing bare floorboards everywhere in Chile and I was shocked at the opulence of the Western lifestyle.

Whenever I visited my mother, who was an extremely generous lady, she always got excited about taking me shopping. She had money and her tastes were extravagant and nothing gave her more pleasure than buying expensive presents for people, especially her family. She prided herself on having the best and she wanted the same for her children. I would arrive home from the mission field in my well worn, plain clothes and she would say, "Let's go shopping. I want to buy you something really lovely." But I could never face going back with something I knew I wouldn't wear, so I would always refuse to go with her and I would watch as her face fell with disappointment.

Looking back at this now I realise that I was being legalistic and was silly to look down my nose at what I perceived as my mother's "materialism". I regretted denying her the pleasure of treating me, but there is no use in saying, "If only I had done things differently . . ." The past is the past and we have to release it.

Letting go of regret

Regrets can be major, like Margaret's and her remorse over her son, or they can be minor, like my issue with my mother, but we need to let go of them just the same. Repentance plays a big part in unburdening ourselves.

Repentance is a form of relinquishment, a letting go of something that has been weighing us down. When we sin we often feel sad, fed up and angry with ourselves, remorseful over what we have done, and we continue to feel that way until we repent and hand over the burden to God. The Greek word for repentance is *metanoia*, which means a change or reversal of mind, but it is more than just a change of mind. Real repentance is a change of behaviour. You decide to turn around and walk in a different direction, in a different way. Repentance is seen by the fruit it produces in our lives – lasting change.

Scott Peck, the psychiatrist and author of *The Road Less Travelled*, was once playing a game of chess with his daughter that proved to be a turning point in his life. He wanted to spend quality time with her that evening before she went to bed. They only had half an hour for the game because his daughter had an exam the next day and wanted to get to bed early that night. However, as they began to play, Peck's strongly competitive streak got the better of him and he became determined to win the game. He took a long time considering every move he made, much to the annoyance of his daughter, so that she began complaining, "Daddy, hurry up. I need to go to bed!" But he carried on taking a long time and in the end his daughter jumped up and cried out, "Oh, for goodness sake, just win the stupid game!" and flew out of the room and went to bed in tears.

Scott Peck realised that he had failed miserably to act like an adult and a good parent and he actually went through a time of depression because one thing had become very clear to him: somehow he had to give up the desire he had to win all the time. This is what he wrote about the experience:

> "That part of me is gone now. It died. It had to die, I killed it. I killed it with my desire to win at parenting. When I was a

child my desire to win at games served me well. As a parent I recognised that it got in my way, so it had to go. I just killed it."

This is a really good example of repentance which leads to relinquishment and a change of behaviour. Repentance is more than an isolated act, it is a way of life, an integral part of Christian living.

One problem with regret is that, unlike Scott Peck, we are often faced with something we have done which we cannot undo. It's too late now for me to behave differently with my mother because she has passed away. I no longer have the opportunity of visiting her in north Devon and saying, "Come on, Mum, I'd love to go shopping with you." But if I have truly repented of that behaviour then there should still be some change in me. It may be too late to make amends with my mother, but I don't have to repeat that behaviour. I don't have to perpetuate that legalistic, poverty mindset any more so that I repeat it in another setting. Peck would have repeated his behaviour again and again if he hadn't decided it needed to die. Repentance always means change.

Repentance as a lifestyle, however, does not mean beating ourselves up the whole time. We need to cultivate the ability to forgive ourselves just as God forgives us. When we sin we tend to think that we ought to be punished and if God isn't going to punish us because of His grace and mercy, then we will punish ourselves, beating ourselves with a big stick and refusing to let ourselves off the hook. But forgiveness is a gift from God to His beloved children and receiving it is like a gift. We just have to receive it, we cannot say, "It's not enough for me." That is the same as saying, "I'm sorry Jesus, Your death actually wasn't sufficient for me. It's OK for other people, but not for me – I have to also pay a bit for what I've done." But if we have repented of our sin, then God has forgiven us. The sin has gone and we have to let go of it. That is part of our relinquishment – giving up beating ourselves.

If you are suffering from regrets of the past, bring them to God and ask Him to take your burden. Repent and forgive anyone you need to forgive and ask God to help you to stop looking backwards and start to look forwards into His plans and purposes for your life.

Summary

Jesus paid for our freedom in full at the cross and it is a gift freely given to us by grace. But there is a cost to freedom for us – that is the cost of letting go of things in our lives that will prevent us from fully taking hold of it. The rich young ruler who came seeking Jesus was unwilling to let go of all the things his wealth provided for him.

One of the things we persistently hang on to is the "if onlys" of life – yesterday's regrets – which prevent us from moving forward into greater freedom.

We need to learn to let go of regret and, again, repentance plays a vital part in the process.

Dealing with the Past ... and the Future

Past hurts

Another hindrance to our freedom in Christ that, like regret, has to do with events in our past, is that of past hurts that still linger in our lives today. I meet many people who are still struggling with hurts they received in the past at somebody else's hands. I recently met a woman who was still very bitter and angry with her husband who had walked out on her twenty years previously and left her to bring up two small children. Maybe we are suffering because of something that happened to us in our childhood or because of some offence that happened to us last week. Either way, unless it is resolved, hurt like this will cause unwanted repercussions in our life that will limit our freedom. We can never simply "bury" stuff and ignore it, because it will always rebound on us at some point.

Past hurt can leave us with a fear of commitment, fear of failure and of trying new things, pain, anxiety and depression.

Some time ago, whilst on a car journey, I listened to *Desert Island Discs* on the radio and the guest was Oliver Postgate who made many popular children's TV programmes throughout a long career in television. He was an elderly man of around eighty and he said something very sad: "I feel always that I am a guest on the planet. I don't exist unless I am working. I am a general nuisance. It isn't until very recently that I have really understood why I have always felt like this and always have to be doing something to prove that I am worthy to be alive."

His childhood had been very well-to-do and he was always surrounded by wealth, but at the same time he had been utterly neglected by his parents. He had grown up believing that it was his fault that no one was interested in him or cared for him, as children are predisposed to do, and the damage that was done to him had been irreversible.

Past hurt can leave us with bitterness and resentment that can eat away inside us like a cancer. I once counselled a lady in her mid-fifties who was still furious about something her mother did to her when she was just three years old. After talking to her briefly the anger soon bubbled up to the surface. Fifty years on she was still rehearsing this hurt as if it had happened the day before and she was incredibly depressed. Unforgiveness never hurts or punishes the perpetrator of the hurt, it only hurts us. Forgiveness is always the final resolution that leads to healing. When we forgive we cancel any debt we feel we are owed and we transfer the responsibility to God for any punishment that He feels should be meted out.

When we make the decision to forgive someone for hurting us, we have to remember that our will travels by express train, whereas our feelings go by slow freight. When you first forgive someone you may not feel very much in your heart; you may still feel that anger and frustration inside you; but your feelings will catch up as soon as you are determined that you will go God's way and do the forgiving that you need to do.

Shattered dreams

Another problem to do with the past is that of shattered dreams. All of us have dreams in lives: dreams for ourselves, dreams for our spouses or our families, our children, or our work. Whether they are realistic or not, if those dreams fail it can make us feel heart-broken and depressed. Maybe our daughter becomes anorexic or our son, who had so much promise, falls in with a bad crowd and seems to be wasting his life away. Maybe we fail to get the promotion at work we so hoped for or our business fails and we go bankrupt. All of these things can tie us up emotionally and stifle our spiritual growth.

Proverbs 13:12 says,

> *"Hope deferred makes the heart sick,*
> *but a longing fulfilled is a tree of life."*

The Message version of that verse begins, *"Unrelenting disappointment leaves you heartsick . . . "* Shattered dreams leave us with the same sense of loss as bereavement and we are faced with working through that loss just as if a person we love has died. But the temptation is always there to avoid doing our "grief work" and take a detour. We have a tendency to try to put off grief and go into protective mode to shield ourselves from the feelings of pain.

There are many detours one can take to avoid grief, but here are three very common ones:

1. Switching off

"Switching off" is when we tell ourselves, "That's it, I'm never going to fall in love again..." or "I'll never allow myself to trust in people so foolishly again..." When we have been hurt we try to limit the possibility of it ever happening again, so we endeavour to control our environment as much as we can to prevent it. Another form of switching off is when we refuse to try something new because we might fail, just because we tried something in the past and failed and don't want to be humiliated again.

2. Dead ends

We go on a "dead end" detour when we put ourselves in that awful place of constantly asking, "Why, Lord? Why did You let that happen?" It is a dead end because we are asking questions that can never be answered. "Why does God allow bad things to happen to good people?" is a question that countless theologians have tried to answer. I call all such questions "Tsunami questions", i.e. why did God allow the Tsunami? I don't believe such questions can ever be answered to our satisfaction. The author Mark Buchanan writes, "The book of Job tells us that suffering is a mystery, and no clear, cut-and-dried theological explanation exists for it that we can come up with in our lifetime." [1] Because they are not answerable such questions trap us in a spiritual dead end.

The antidote to this dead end is trust. We need to come to the place where we can say, "God, I don't understand, but I do trust You." God and His purposes are way beyond our understanding. If we try to understand God we are doing nothing more than trying to squeeze Him into a little box the size of our minds. We like to try and figure God out and create formulas to explain how He works, but we will never do it. We have a revelation of who our God is in Scripture, but the fact is He is much bigger than that! He is bigger than anything we can possibly imagine, so it is pointless getting stuck in the dead end of "why?"

3. The gap filler

The third common detour people take to avoid dealing with loss is the "gap filler". We rush off to take hold of anything we think will fill up the gap that the loss has left. We keep ourselves busy and go from this thing to that so that we don't have time to experience any bad feelings.

But loss has to be properly dealt with whether it is due to regret, past hurt or shattered dreams. We have to come to a place of acceptance and then let it go, placing it in God's hands.

The author Barbara Johnson, who wrote many humorous books, had four sons. She lost two of them: one in Vietnam and the other at the hands of a drunk driver. Then a third son was lost to her for seven years into a homosexual lifestyle. She grieved for her son and carried that burden to such a degree that she was almost ready to be sectioned, she was so distraught and depressed. One day she felt so tired and exhausted with carrying the grief of her boy that she just gave him up and relinquished him to God. This is what she wrote about her experience:

> "That was the key. I personally surrendered my hopes, my plans, my life, my son. I realised I was powerless to fix him, to bring him back or change him. Only God's touch on Larry's life could do any of that. I finally understood that all I could do was let him go, turn him over to God and let Him work in Larry's life."[2]

Seven years passed and eventually her son came back home and asked her and God's forgiveness. As Barbara commented, "Pain is inevitable, but misery is optional."

Allowing God to heal our past

Letting go of regret, hurt and shattered dreams is essential if we are to move on in our Christian lives. The great thing is, as soon as we release our burden to God it opens up the possibility of His healing in our lives.

God wants to touch us and heal us and His healing can take place in a myriad different ways. There are many different ministries out there who deal with inner healing and they are like tools in a toolbox. God will pick out the right tool to fix you because He knows you and knows exactly how you need to be healed. Sometimes it can be through a dream, a word that someone speaks to you, a verse of Scripture that God uses to speak to you in a way you've never understood before; sometimes the process will happen quickly and at other times it will be a long process. Our job is simply to be open to God's healing and to come to Him. We must not wait to deal with things, but start today dealing with our issues.

I love the story of Peter's healing and restoration in John's Gospel. As Jesus was arrested and taken for trial Peter denied knowing Him three times as he was warming his hands over a fire in the early morning chill. A young girl identified him as being one of Jesus' followers and he strongly denied it. As he did, a cock crowed, just as Jesus had predicted, and Peter went out and wept bitterly. He was a broken man. He had said so many big things to Jesus: "I'll never leave You ... I'll never deny You ... " then he had crumbled when confronted even by a little maid. He was absolutely shattered by his failure.

Then, in one of His post-resurrection appearances, Jesus turns up on the beach one morning while the disciples are just finishing an unsuccessful fishing trip. They have been out all night and have caught nothing. Jesus calls to them, "Friends, haven't you any fish?" At first the disciples don't realise that it's Jesus and they just call back, "No." Then He tells them that if they cast their net on the other side of the boat they will catch some fish. *"When they did, they were unable to haul the net in because of the large number of fish"* (John 21:6). At this point they realise it's the Lord and impetuous Peter leaps out of the boat into the water and rushes to the beach.

Jesus has built a fire on the beach in order to cook them some breakfast. It's like He is recreating the scene of Peter's failure. They are gathered around the fire warming themselves and Jesus asks Peter three times, *"Simon son of John, do you truly love me ... ?"* (John 21:15). Three times Peter has to respond, "You know that I love you" and then Jesus reinstates him and re-commissions him saying, *"Then feed my sheep."* It is as though Jesus has taken that bad memory, recreated the scene of Peter's failure and then overwritten it with God's intended purpose for his life.

A young man once told me about a wonderful healing experience he'd had. Some people had been praying for him that God would heal a deep hurt from his past that had resulted from his abusive father. God took him back in his memory to a time when he was about seven years old. He was in the kitchen at home and his dad was yelling at him. His father was always verbally abusive towards him and he was shouting, "You're no good, you're a loser. You'll never amount to anything." Suddenly he was aware of Jesus standing near to him in the kitchen. His father couldn't see Jesus but the young man could see Him. Jesus turned to him and spoke, saying, "In My kingdom there are no losers and you belong in My kingdom." Jesus took that terrible memory and wrote over the top of it. At that moment my young friend received an incredible healing touch from God.

Mark Buchanan says, "God has set a limit to His power. Not even He can remove the past and the past comes bearing its wounds. What God does is better. He redeems the past *and* its wounds." Letting go of past regrets does not mean forgetting the past, shutting the door on it, or putting up a "no fishing" sign. All these are unhealthy ways of dealing with the past. The past is part of us, a bit of who we are, but we must not allow it to define us. Nor can we allow it to dictate our future or hold us back in any way. We have to appropriately resolve it, deal with it and let it go.

Tomorrow's anxieties – the "what ifs" of life

Dr Richard Gantz, in his book *The Secret of Self-Control*, says that,

> "Regardless of its source anxiety results in physical and spiritual destruction. It will tear you up, consume you, your time, your energy, your thoughts and your life. It will remove you from

the present in which you can exercise some control and experience joy, and move you into an uncertain future over which you have no control. Anxiety will direct you away from the unchanging character of God towards your frailties."[3]

Proverbs 12:25 says,

"An anxious heart weighs a man down . . . "

As well as the problems of the past, worrying about the future can be just as debilitating. All kinds of things worry us: family matters, health, education, relationships, our neighbours, our finances. Money is a big one: will we be able to pay our mortgage? Will we have enough money for the future? What if we get into debt?

I profess to be an expert on the subject of worry – an expert in worrying and an expert in looking for answers to it! Therefore I can tell you we must learn to let go of anxiety and trust God to take care of our future just as He can take care of our past. I offer the following advice to help us relinquish anxiety:

1. If there is any action you can take, then take it

If you are worried about money, for instance, then find somebody who understands finances and talk to them. Go and get help. If you have discovered a lump on your body, don't ignore it, go and speak to your doctor. Don't allow the old excuse, "he/she will think I'm being stupid" to prevent you, go and get checked out. It is much better to get peace of mind than to go on worrying. Be prayerful about it but do take action. Seek God and seek advice from those you trust.

2. Pray specifically

Sometimes there is no action you can take. You may have something that is weighing you down but there is no possibility of action. How do we handle that kind of anxiety? The first and most obvious thing is to pray and read the Bible. You may groan and think, "Well, I've done that. Of course I read my Bible and pray all the time." But just think for a moment about how you do it. Philippians 4:6 says,

> *"Do not be anxious about anything, but in everything, by prayer and petition, with thanksgiving, present your requests to God."*

The first thing to remember is that we have to be specific with our prayers. If you can, tell God exactly what it is you are anxious about. There are occasions when I have what I call "free floating" anxiety. I don't always know what it is I'm anxious about, I just feel uncomfortable. At those times I ask God, "Lord, why am I feeling like this? What is it that's bothering me?" and then I sit and wait. I don't think there has ever been a time when God hasn't shown me what it is and then it can be dealt with.

3. Pray kingdom prayers

As well as praying specifically, we need to "think kingdom" when we pray and not get wrapped up in ourselves. Say, for instance, that we have a problem with our boss at work and the situation is making us anxious. It's OK to pray, "Oh God, my boss is really getting me down. He/she is such a pain in the neck! Lord, I really wish You would remove them." God understands those kind of prayers which are born out of frustration. But I suggest you get beyond that and pray kingdom orientated prayers.

Kingdom prayers have much more of eternity attached to them and are not short-term and self-seeking. "Get rid of my boss" type prayers are transient and don't seek to achieve anything for the good of the kingdom. Yet Jesus said, *"Seek first his kingdom and his righteousness, and all these things will be given to you as well"* (Matthew 6:33). It is far better then to pray, "God, I don't know how this will work out, but please help me to act in a godly way towards this person. Lord, bring good out of a bad situation. Give me Your power and strength and help me find ways of blessing my boss who is being such a pain in the neck." You can be sure that God will be in that kind of prayer and will begin showing you things to do that will result in Him being glorified.

4. Pray for God's will to be done
We can also pray what Jesus told us to pray: *"Your will be done."* Some may say that's an opt out, but no, it's how Jesus instructed us to pray, *"Your kingdom come, your will be done"* (Matthew 6:10). When we pray that we are praying the kingdom into our situation.

Some people seem to believe that God's will is a mysterious thing and cannot be known, but this is not true and contradicts God's character. We are God's children, we belong to Him, and good fathers communicate with their children. Jesus calls us His "friends" and friends communicate with one another. So when we pray *"Your will be done"* we should ask God, "Lord, show me what Your will is so I can pray it in . . . what is Your will for my son who I'm so worried about? . . . what is Your will in my work situation?" Then wait and let God show us what it is.

The author Bill Johnson talks in his books about "leaning into God" – leaning a little closer to Him in order to hear Him better. Sometimes my husband, David, speaks very softly and I have to lean towards him to hear what he is saying. That's what we are meant to do with God. Once we have asked Him a question we need to lean in and wait for Him to speak.

If, at times, we really don't know what to pray and God doesn't seem to be saying anything, we can always pray in tongues. It's a simple gift that God has provided for our edification. Paul writes,

"In the same way, the Spirit helps us in our weakness. We do not know what we ought to pray for, but the Spirit himself intercedes for us with groans that words cannot express."   (Romans 8:26)

God has provided for us to such an extent that when we are at a loss for words the Holy Spirit helps us and intercedes for us "without words".

5. Pray with thanksgiving

Prayer that is full of thanksgiving is a great antidote to anxiety. Bill Johnson says, "Focus on what God has done, not on what He hasn't done." We have a tendency when we pray to say, "O God, I've been praying for this for ages and You haven't answered me yet." Instead of focusing on this we need to focus on and praise God for the things He has done. Johnson says, "We disarm hell through thanksgiving and thanksgiving keeps us sane and alive."

Proverbs 17:22 says,

"A joyful heart is good medicine ... '   (NASB)

There is power in thanksgiving. If I am worried at night, which is when I tend to worry about things and turn them over in my mind, I start praising God and thanking Him. I make a list of thanksgiving in my mind and I start going through all those things that I'm thankful for. Usually by the time I've gotten through half the list, I'm asleep, because the list is so long!

Paul writes in Philippians 4:4, *"Rejoice in the Lord always. I will say it again: Rejoice!"* Just as repentance is a way of life for the Christian, so too is thanksgiving. We should, of all people, be the most thankful; constantly thankful to God for the good things He has given us. It's a beautiful thing to see grateful people because there is something very attractive about them. Make thankfulness a habit and when trials come you will already be in the habit of giving thanks.

6. Give your burden to Jesus

Finally, the advice of Peter is,

> *"Cast all your anxiety on him because he cares for you."*
> (1 Peter 5:7)

And Jesus Himself invites us to,

> *"Come to me, all you who are weary and burdened, and I will give you rest."*   (Matthew 11:28)

We have to learn to relinquish the things that burden us, and we may have to do so again and again. You know how it is: we give God our anxieties and then we take them right back again. Well, keep doing it until one day you find you have left it with the Lord for good.

Jesus said,

> *"Do not worry about your life . . . Who of you by worrying can add a single hour to his life? . . . Therefore do not worry about tomorrow, for tomorrow will worry about itself. Each day has enough trouble of its own."*   (Matthew 6:25, 27, 34)

What is God wanting you to release right now? What do you need to let go of? Is it regret, shame, disappointment, hurt, worry or anxiety that is robbing you of some of your freedom?

If we do the work of relinquishment then the Bible promises in Philippians 4:7,

> *"The peace of God, which transcends all understanding, will guard your hearts and your minds in Christ Jesus."*

That is real freedom.

Summary

Another hindrance to our freedom in Christ is past regrets, the shadow of which have a very real effect on our present living. Anger and bitterness can be lurking in our lives and can be brought to the surface by the right trigger. Past hurt can leave us with a fear of commitment and this will hinder our fully trusting in God.

Shattered dreams are another problem from our past that hinder our progress. *"Hope deferred makes the heart sick"* and unfulfilled dreams, whether realistic or not, can leave us with depression. We need to deal with the "grief" of shattered dreams just as if we'd lost a loved one. Beware of taking one of the following "detours" to avoid dealing with the issue:

1. Switching off and saying, "I will never trust again."
2. Getting trapped in the dead end of constantly asking, "Why?"
3. Trying to fill the gap of loss with numerous other things.

Letting go of our burdens will open us up to God's healing. Jesus has the ability to "recreate" the scene of our past hurts and "override" them with His truth and heal us as He did for Peter.

As well as the problems of the past we need to address our anxiety about the future – the "what ifs" of life. Uncertainty and anxiety can be very harmful to us. In order to relinquish anxiety we can take the following action:

1. If there is any action you can take, take it.
2. Pray specifically about the issues that are concerning you.
3. Think "kingdom" when you pray and avoid "get rid of my boss" prayers.
4. Ask God for insight into His will for the situation and then pray into it.
5. Pray with thanksgiving.
6. Give your burden to Jesus.

Notes

1. Source: http://markbuchanan.net
2. Barbara Johnson, *Where Does a Mother Go to Resign?*, Thomas Nelson Inc.
3. Richard Gantz, *The Secret of Self-Control*, Crossway Books, 1998.

CHAPTER

7

The Cost of Letting Go

Once, while David and I lived in Chile, an evangelist from Central America came down to conduct an evangelistic campaign in a local football stadium. On the first night of the event I went along with a friend to see what was happening and I was absolutely staggered. I had never seen anything like it. For a start, the evangelist himself was truly Pentecostal and spent most of the evening yelling into the microphone! But, at the end of his talk he declared, "Tonight God is going to heal deaf people. If you are deaf, stand up, God is healing you right now." Lots of people stood and then he said, "If anyone has been healed come down to the front."

At that moment a young man who was sitting right behind me jumped up and went bounding down the aisle to the front. I watched him go and thought, "My goodness, I know that young man, he's one of the members of our church. He is deaf." And sure enough, God had healed this boy and he had received his hearing back. I was so excited that I went home to tell David and said, "You've got to come tomorrow night. In fact, we've all got to go, the whole family. This is extraordinary. We are seeing amazing miracles."

At that time we had a girl working with us in the church who had come out from England to spend her summer holidays with us. She was also deaf. David immediately said,

"We've got to ask Susan to come with us. Maybe she'll get healed?" David called her and told her about the event the next evening and offered to pick her up, telling her to wait on the corner of her street at 7.00 pm. The next evening we set off and passed by the end of her street at 7.00 pm, but there was no sign of her. We hung around for a while but she didn't turn up.

When he saw her the following day David spoke to her and mentioned the fact that she hadn't shown up. She explained why and her answer was quite remarkable: "I thought about coming," she said. "Then I thought, 'Say I got healed – who would I be then?'" She had really counted the cost of letting go of something that had become as much a part of her identity as her name. Her deafness had been there her whole life and she wondered, "Who would I be if I wasn't deaf any longer?"

The cost of letting go

There is a real cost involved in letting go of who we are in order to become who God wants us to be. It is a risky business – just like the merchant trader who had to unload all his baggage in order to get his camel through the tiny city gate. What if someone took advantage of him while he was in this exposed, vulnerable state? Similarly, the rich young ruler couldn't bring himself to take the risk of laying down his baggage in order to find out if Jesus alone was enough for him.

But the Bible consistently speaks about letting go in order to embrace what God has for us. Paul writes in Ephesians 4,

> *"You were taught, with regard to your former way of life, to put off your old self, which is being corrupted by its deceitful desires; to be made new in the attitude of your minds; and to put on the new self, created to be like God in true righteousness and holiness."*

(Ephesians 4:22–24)

And elsewhere he writes,

> *"When I was a child, I talked like a child, I thought like a child, I reasoned like a child. When I became a man, I put childish ways behind me."*   (1 Corinthians 13:11)

Our journey to maturity in Christ involves a lot of letting go and laying down. It is a constant feature of our life journey.

When I was a child our family lived right out in the country and there was never anyone around for me to play with. I had lots of "things" to play with and I invented lots of imaginative games, plus there were horses, cats, dogs and rabbits around to occupy me, but there were never any other children around, so I had quite a lonely childhood for the most part. But, when I was around eleven years old, a little boy came to live in the lane near us.

We had never had a family in "the big house", as we called it, who'd had children before. But this army family arrived and they had a little boy of about ten years old. Suddenly I had someone to play with and it was absolutely wonderful. He and I became great friends and we had a fantastic time together climbing trees and playing games.

This lasted for a couple of years, but I was entering adolescence and the appeal of playing the kind of games we used to play began to disappear. Suddenly I wasn't into climbing trees, pretending to be an aeroplane or shooting imaginary enemies any more. It all seemed too childish to me. It was time for me to let go and move on. But it was hard for me to leave that old friend and realise that he wasn't ready to grow up and move on yet.

Letting go is a normal part of our Christian life. There is no freedom without it. We have to let go in order to move on in God's purposes for us. There will be no transformation into the image of Jesus except that we lay down some things we are holding on to. Change is always hard because it involves a bit of us dying. Sometimes it seems like we are losing something that is important to us, but we won't move into the purposes of God still holding onto it.

When Mother Teresa was twelve years old, she told her mother that she wanted to be a nun and her mother told her, "Put your hand into the hand of Jesus and go all the way with Him." What that meant for Mother Teresa was leaving her family, leaving her home country, Macedonia, and going off to Calcutta. At eighteen she joined the Sisters of Loreto, an Irish community of nuns with missions in India and began a job teaching at St Mary's High School in Calcutta. She never saw her family again.

The suffering and poverty she glimpsed outside the convent walls made such a deep impression on her that in 1948 she received permission from her superiors to leave the convent school and devote herself to working among the poorest of the poor in the slums of Calcutta. Although she was clearly walking God's path for her life, Mother Teresa found it desperately difficult to leave the Sisters – just as hard as she had found it to leave her family and her home years before – but she knew it was the right thing to do.

Jesus made some difficult statements regarding letting go. He said,

> "Unless a grain of wheat falls into the ground and dies, it remains only a single seed. But if it dies, it produces many seeds. The man who loves his life will lose it, while the man who hates his life in this world will keep it for eternal life."   (John 12:24–25)

And

> "If anyone would come after me, he must deny himself and take up his cross and follow me. For whoever wants to save his life will lose it, but whoever loses his life for me will find it."
>
> (Matthew 16:24–25)

These are both statements of letting go and laying down. But what does that mean for you and me? Letting go will mean different things at different times for each of us. Some of us may have to give up material possession, but not others. For some it may mean a change of lifestyle or even, like Mother Teresa, moving to a different country far away from our family in our quest to follow Jesus.

For the rich young ruler it was his wealth. That was the thing that Jesus honed in on – his material possessions. I don't believe it was his money that was the problem as much as what it signified for him and that was independence.

The trap of independence

As a Christian, independence is one of our greatest enemies and can cause us all kinds of problems because independent people don't need others. This has been one of the greatest areas of difficulty for me because, having led a solitary childhood, independence has always been the name of the game for me. I really hate the thought of dependence. Recently I had to sign an enduring power of attorney document due to a new Government ruling. I pray I'll never need to use it, but at the time it felt as though I was signing my life away. How could I possibly sign this thing that means at some point somebody else is going to make decisions for me?

I grew up very proud of my independence. If, when you really need help in life, there is no one around for you to rely on then you tell yourself, "What's the point of needing other people? What's the point of being dependent on somebody?" I grew up commending myself for not being "one of those people", as I saw it, who needs someone around all the time to pat them on the head and tell them they're doing alright. I was proud of the fact that I could manage on my own. But then I met my friend Prue Bedwell.

We are now the best of friends, but at that time, before our friendship had begun to blossom, we had worked together just a few times. On one of these occasions Prue said to me, "You're very hard to know, Mary, really hard to get to know." I replied, "Really? Well, the fact is, I don't really need other people, you know." Surprised by my answer Prue said, "Oh, really? Well, that's not very biblical is it?" It was my turn to be surprised. I pulled myself up to my full height (which is not nearly as tall as she is) and said a bit crossly, "What do you mean?" Prue said to me, "Why don't you go home and read John 17 where Jesus talks about us being one?"

I did and to my horror I thought, "Oh my goodness, she's right." No one had ever challenged me like that before and I realised that independence isn't right for a Christian. We are not meant to be independent, but *interdependent* with one another. We are all in this together.

I remember Juan Carlos Ortiz, an Argentinian preacher, once talking about mashed potatoes and new potatoes. You boil new potatoes and serve them up whole with their skins still on. But, he said, Christians are meant to be like mashed potatoes. We have our skins removed and we are all mashed in together! Independence just doesn't work in the Christian life. You cannot be mixed into God's family and still be independent. Dependency is part of the package when we become Christians. There can be no real fruitfulness or freedom in our lives without it. Jesus says in John 15:5, *"Apart from me you can do nothing."* I think we read that verse and think, "Come on, Lord, surely we can do something?" But no, Jesus says, nothing of eternal value.

Sometimes I scare myself with what I call my "fall back" mentality. When I'm not thinking, not hooked into God, and someone asks me to do something, I find it so easy to say "yes" and immediately rely on my own abilities, my own talents, my expertise and experience, instead of asking God for His help and His wisdom. The rich young ruler had plenty to fall back on and I believe Jesus was challenging him to strip all of this away so that he could find out who he really was underneath. The young man enjoyed material security; his money would have given him popularity, importance, status. He had a sense of worth, significance, and the freedom to do what he wanted, when he wanted, how he wanted. He had rights, rights that other people didn't have. But all that he had, he possessed independently of God.

He had a lot to lose. Imagine: he's rich, he's young and he's a ruler. He's very important and he's got a lot going for him. Then he meets a poor, itinerant Galilean (Galileans were generally considered to be hillbillies from way up north), an insignificant preacher who's got no money, uncertain parentage and no Rabbi training behind Him. Is he going to follow that man?

And what about joining the disciples? Again, a bunch of hillbillies, fishermen, tax collectors, men of ill repute, a motley crew, a group of men who didn't have any belongings and no idea where they were going to lay their heads. Was he really going to give up all he had for that?

Michael Crosby says, "The kingdom of God can only be received by empty hands." Jesus put the challenge before this young man but he just could not let go of his independence and in so doing he missed the greatest adventure of his life. Let's look more closely at the things this young man was unwilling to let go of which caused him to miss out on God's blessing:

Security

Because of his wealth this man had security independently of God. It meant that he never had to think about catering for his basic human needs, the most fundamental of which, after food and water, are shelter and security.

What gives us security in life? Usually it revolves around people and possessions. Having loved ones around us gives a sense of security. We depend on people and draw strength from them. Financially, we want to know that we have enough to live on and to do things with, to keep ourselves and our family fed and watered and have the occasional holiday.

But when we think about these things, that most people depend on for their security, they are actually pretty insecure and flimsy. Neither people nor possessions are consistently reliable and they can easily be stripped away leaving us exposed and insecure. If all our security is invested in our money, what happens if we lose it all and have nothing? And if our security is drawn from people we love, what happens when those people are no longer there?

Of course, there is nothing wrong with loving your spouse, your family, and having good friends around you. There is nothing wrong with having possessions or knowing that you have a good pension in the future. But we have to ask ourselves the question: deep down what or whom are we really depending upon for our security? Are we building our lives on the firm foundation of a relationship with God, or on temporal things that will pass away in time? The rich young ruler depended on his wealth for his security and missed discovering the greater, the more dependable, eternal security that is available to us in God the Father.

Hudson Taylor, one of the earliest missionaries to China, learned to depend on God for his security when he was still only nineteen. One night he was called out to go and pray with a mother and her children. The mother was desperately ill, her children were also sick. They were absolutely impoverished having no money at all and didn't know where their next meal was coming from. He arrived to pray for them and, he hoped, lead them to Christ. He was just about to open his mouth to pray that God's comfort and help would come to them when He felt God say to him, "You hypocrite!" Taylor had a silver coin in his pocket and he knew that the money would help to alleviate their suffering. He felt literally unable to pray for this family while the coin was still in his pocket, so he took it out, gave it to the mother and then prayed for them. Afterwards he went home knowing he had given away the last bit of money he had. He now had no money and all he had at home was enough oats to make himself one bowl of porridge to eat the following day. That was it.

The next morning he made himself the porridge and sat there wondering what to do. He now had no money in his pocket and no food in his cupboard. Then he heard the plop of an envelope dropping through his letterbox. He opened it and inside was a single gold coin that was worth ten times the value of the silver coin he had given away. At that moment he triumphantly cried out, "That's good interest! Invested in God's bank for twelve hours and it brings me in this! That's the bank for me." From that time on and throughout his life he continued to put his trust in God's provision for his security and God never let him down. The young ruler missed out on experiencing the interest that God's bank would have paid him if he had invested his wealth in it. He missed out on the loving care and security of God the Father, the God who owns the cattle on a thousand hills.

Security is a big issue for all of us, but especially for those who have been let down in the past. If we have experienced insecurity as a child, or bad things have happened to us, then we may find it difficult to trust completely in God. But we must not be tempted to try and grab bits of security from here and there in order to feel better. We have to work at trusting God more and more. People and possessions will come and go throughout our life, but if our roots are planted deep into our relationship with God then we won't be thrown off track.

In the next chapter we will continue to look at the issues of independence that troubled the rich young ruler and prevented him from fully trusting God.

Summary

There is a cost to letting go of both past hurts and anxiety about the future and fully trusting God for our life, but letting go is a normal part of life and our development into Christian maturity.

The temptation for us is to protect our independence and to use our own resources to provide for our basic needs in life. The rich young ruler had all the components of his basic needs met, but he possessed them independently of God:

Security

The first and most fundamental need we have is for security. We tend to rely on people and possessions to provide us with security, but in reality this will build an unstable foundation for our life. We need to look to God to provide for our need for security.

CHAPTER 8

Trusting God for All Our Emotional Needs

Satisfaction

The rich young ruler also had satisfaction in life, or so he thought, independently from God. There is nothing higher on society's agenda these days than satisfaction. Whenever we switch on the TV, listen to the radio or open a newspaper they are encouraging us to do things to satisfy ourselves, to be fulfilled, to have pleasure. Why? In the words of a well known TV ad, "Because we're worth it"! Haven't you heard that 100 times? I'm so sick and tired of hearing those words on the TV. I know I have worth, but not in the way they are saying.

We are daily faced with the choice of putting God first or putting ourselves first. We gravitate towards those things we think will fulfil us and give us pleasure, but they are not necessarily things that are good for us. We look at things and think, "Yes, I need that to make me happy." We think we should have it, after all, why shouldn't we be satisfied, we've only got one life to live?

The trouble with this mindset is that is that the world promotes satisfaction and getting what we want at any price. For instance, if the husband/wife we are married to has become boring, then the world says it's OK to go and find someone else who is more exciting. After all, it's all about "me" at the end of the day, isn't it? We make some amazing excuses to justify such behaviour. I spoke to a lady a while ago who was doing this exact thing and was trying to tell herself that she had never really loved her husband in the first place, so she owed it to herself to be with someone she loved. On the top of that she had deluded herself into believing that God understood and was perfectly OK with what was happening.

Sam Storms says that,

> "The message trumpeted by the world, the flesh and the devil, is relatively simple. It is often packaged in different shapes and sounds, but the underlying theme is monotonously the same. Like a reverberating echo in an empty cage, the refrain is incessant, unending and unchanging: there is more joy in illicit sex than in Jesus; there is more joy in goodies and gold than in Jesus; there is more joy in power and pride and a drug-induced high than in Jesus; there is more joy in looking fit and feeling good and the latest fashion than in Jesus."

There is an addictive, magnetic pull to seek pleasure, happiness, excitement and success in the wrong way that will beckon to you throughout your Christian life. We need to be alert to it to resist it. Those of us who are married are bound to meet people who are more attractive than our spouses. It is inevitable. All of us, as we get older, grow a bit baggy and saggy! Temptation will beckon and the argument taking place in our head will be, "I deserve a little bit of excitement and happiness." We must remember, it is not worth sacrificing all we have for a bit of fleeting pleasure. I have seen so much heartbreak and so many kids' lives messed up just because one parent has looked for that "little bit of satisfaction". We live a very short life on this earth, but we have eternity to spend with God. Only He can totally satisfy us.

The scripture Jeremiah 2:13, that I mentioned earlier, should be underlined in everyone's Bible. It is one of the most important in Scripture:

"My people have committed two sins:
They have forsaken me,
*   the spring of living water . . . "*

God is the only One who can satisfy all our needs, for security, for satisfaction and fulfilment. People will go this way and that looking for satisfaction, but actually God is the One who can give us the biggest buzz of our lives.

I remember when John Wimber came to visit our church back in 1981. At the time David was about to embark on a PhD. He had already studied for his MPhil and wanted to do his PhD on the history of Chile, on which he is an expert. But when John Wimber came and taught us how to minister to people in the power of the Spirit, we were both so excited that David said to me, "I want to do this till the day I die!" and he flung the idea of his PhD out the window. He knew that he couldn't pursue both. It would have been nice for him to be "Dr Pytches", but so what? It would last for a few years and then we're in eternity. If we get hooked into God now and immerse ourselves in the business of His kingdom we will get the greatest satisfaction we could ever have.

The rich young ruler missed out on the excitement of seeing Jesus raising people from the dead. He missed seeing Jesus Himself raised from the dead! He could possibly have been there in the upper room at Pentecost when the Holy Spirit came for the very first time. Or maybe he could have found himself travelling the world with the Apostle Paul.

Many things in life promise us satisfaction, but Psalm 16 says,

"You have made known to me the path of life;
*   you will fill me with joy in your presence,*
*   with eternal pleasures at your right hand."*   (verse 11)

We can't afford to miss that because we looked for some temporary, transient bit of satisfaction.

Kathryn Kuhlman, who had an amazing ministry of signs and wonders, went through a period in her life where she turned her back on the satisfaction God gives and tried her own approach. She had a relationship with a man she should never have gotten involved with and it led her away from God. Six years later she was out for a walk one day when she saw a sign that said "Dead End". As she looked at the sign she was suddenly filled with heartache for what she was missing – the wonderful touch of the Holy Spirit on her life. She missed the spiritual power that she had moved in previously. Right there she prayed this prayer: "Dear Jesus, I surrender all. I give it all to You. Take my body, take my heart, all I am is Yours."

Within months she was back preaching to thousands. She reached multiple thousands of people with God's message of salvation and healing. People would even get healed in the queue outside waiting to come into her meetings, such was the anointing God had placed on her.

Let's not miss out because we are chasing after things that in the end don't satisfy us. They are insubstantial shadows, but God is the reality.

Identity

As my husband, David, is fond of saying, this man was rich, young and a ruler. That was his identity. Who would he be without those defining attributes? Like our friend, Susan, who did not know who she would be without her deafness, I think the young man's identity was so wrapped up in his wealth and power that he simply could not imagine life as a poor disciple. Who would he be then? With his riches and power he was a "somebody".

We all need to have a unique identity. We all have a name that identifies us, a family, an occupation, associations with church or other organisations, and all that is perfectly normal. But often we lean too heavily on those things to give us our sense of self-worth. At other times, because we don't feel that our identity is "good enough" for some reason, we latch onto things to make us feel good about ourselves, things that will make us feel significant. It might be an activity, something we do or a talent we have. Or our identity may be wrapped up in our association with another person, so that when someone says to us, "Who are you?" we respond, "Oh, I'm so and so's wife . . . daughter . . . son . . . friend" etc. We may be stating the truth, but we can't use that label as our identity. If that label did not exist we would still be a somebody in God's sight.

One of the things that happened to me when I retired was that I crashed headlong into the "Who am I?" issue once again. I had been a clergyman's wife and done all the stuff that goes along with that. I didn't even realise I had done it, but I had clung on to the label of "vicar's wife". I knew I could sit on my own in church and people would always come and seek me out to talk to me. Suddenly I found myself in church and nobody wanted to seek me out, I was just sitting there! So I decided to write a book about it called *Who Am I?* One of the blessings of doing that book, besides finding out who I really was, was a list I compiled at the back of all the Bible verses relating to who God says we are. You can read it at the end of the book.

Many of us have struggled with a negative self-identity as we have grown up. I struggled with one for years. To overcome it I needed God to speak into my life the truth about who I really am in Christ. In His sight I was no accident. He knew me when I was in my mother's womb. He planned for me. He had a meaning and a purpose for my life. In His kingdom I am a "somebody", chosen and beloved. Each of us needs to find that out for ourselves.

Just like our quest for satisfaction, if we try to root our identity in anything other than God it will be transient and short-lived. The rich young ruler's identity was so wrapped up in his wealth and power that he missed being a friend of Jesus, a chosen and beloved person, part of a royal priesthood. He missed hearing the voice of the Father saying, "I'm well pleased with you son", that would have truly affirmed and established his identity forever.

We all need that kind of affirmation. We may never have had an earthly father who affirmed us, who put his arm around us and said, "Well done, son" or "This is my girl", but God can do that for us and establish our identity as His beloved child. I have watched my twelve grandchildren go through puberty with their hormones all over the place, struggling with spotty faces and other traumas common to teenagers. They need someone who will regularly put their arm around them and say, "I'm really proud of you! You're doing great" or to be the voice of calm and reason saying, "It's going to be OK, you'll come through this."

When one of my granddaughters entered puberty her dad said, "Right, today we're really going to celebrate" and they went off on a shopping trip. She was in heaven! They set aside the whole day and he spent a lot of money on her. In fact, whatever she set her eyes on he was buying it. It was his way of saying, "I'm so proud of you, you've become a woman today."

Without the affirmation of our Father God we will have an empty hole inside us that needs to be filled. If we don't turn to Jesus for affirmation then we will be constantly looking to others to affirm us, always looking for people to say, "Well done ... great job." It's nice when others affirm us, but the truth is, it is never enough. What we really need is for our heavenly Father to speak His affirmation over us saying, "This is My boy ... My girl ... chosen and beloved."

I remember the night I opened up Colossians and read those words: *"chosen ... and dearly loved"* (Colossians 4:12). I had read them a hundred times before and they had never gone in. That night God moved them from my head to my heart. I said to Him, "You mean I wasn't a mistake?" "No," God replied, "I chose you. You weren't a mistake." At that moment something inside me settled down and relaxed. I knew I no longer had to try to be somebody; I didn't have to make it happen, I didn't have to be a success, I didn't have to go chasing after this or that, because I was God's dearly loved child.

In this truth is where all of our identities lie. If we laid down on the floor and did nothing else for the rest of our lives we would still be chosen and dearly loved children of God.

Acceptance

Someone has said, "Our greatest need is acceptance, our greatest fear is rejection." Rejection is a truly horrible thing. I don't care how secure you are, how wonderful a background you have, how fantastic your parents were, or how well you've done in life, rejection will still be painful for you, as it is for all of us.

The rich young ruler knew acceptance and again, he possessed it independently of God. His riches would have given him a passport to all the best parties in town, the most prestigious banquets. He may have been throwing many of them himself. He was young, rich and powerful. He just couldn't bring himself to give all that up to become an "unacceptable" disciple.

We will do almost anything to avoid being rejected, especially if we have experienced rejection in the past, and almost anything to belong, to be loved, to be appreciated. Some of us do it by being people-pleasers. I know I sometimes do. Do you ever get that feeling where you are almost standing by the side of yourself and you can't believe what you are saying or doing? I shock myself at times by what I say and do in order to be accepted by others.

Sometimes we get into the habit of boasting and bragging, hoping that might win us some admiration from someone. Or else we do that stupid thing of not ever being able to say no.

Either approach means that we will be constantly driven by a desire to please others and live up to their expectations of us in order to feel accepted.

What about wearing masks? Do you wear a mask so that people only see the nice bit of you? Sometimes we disguise the real us because we feel that if others knew what we were really like they would reject us. So we put on a false veneer, "Praise the Lord, everything is wonderful, thank you." We would never admit that we had a row with our husband/wife on the way to church, or that our kids sometimes behave very badly. Instead we wear the mask of what we believe to be the "acceptable us".

But the result of mask wearing is that you miss out on enjoying real intimacy with people. You miss out on people really knowing you and there is such a relief when people really "know" and love you for who you are, because then you can truly relax and just be yourself. David and I go on holiday with our good friends Richard and Prue Bedwell every year as we have done for the last fifteen years. We travel together, live in a little apartment somewhere abroad and are in close quarters for two weeks. We know each other in and out, every little foible, and there is something so liberating about that. It's nice to be known, to know people's habits and the things they like and don't like, and to be able to tease them about it sometimes and have a laugh.

The rich young ruler missed out on finding true acceptance – to know and be known by God the Father – and he somehow could not bring himself to answer the call of Jesus. The Bible says he went away sad. I wonder what happened to his life after that? It is so easy to get trapped by the short-term, transient things of life that, compared to eternity, are so fleeting and temporal. It's very easy to get caught in some of the traps that the rich young ruler got caught in. Dallas Willard once described sin as "not wanting to miss out". In other words, "will Jesus be enough for me?" That was exactly the trap the rich young ruler got caught in – will Jesus be enough to meet my needs for acceptance? Sadly he decided against risking everything he had to follow Jesus. Had he "lost" his life for the kingdom he would have truly found it.

After the rich young ruler left, Peter said to Jesus, *"We have left everything to follow you!"* and Jesus responded with the following:

> *"I tell you the truth . . . no one who has left home or wife or brothers or parents or children for the sake of the kingdom of God will fail to receive many times as much in this age and, in the age to come, eternal life."*   (Luke 18:29–30)

Relinquishing the concerns that crowd our lives is never easy, because dying is not easy. Whether we are dying to self or releasing some of the things we have discussed throughout this book, it is hard to leave and move on. But if we will just trust God for all our needs, emotional or otherwise, and surrender to His purposes for our lives we will know the greatest degree of freedom anyone could know. Dwight L. Moody once said, "The world has yet to see what God can do with a man or woman who is wholly committed to Him."

We must keep our eyes fixed on Jesus, upon the eternal and not the temporal. With eternal life we are going to move into something incredible and the more we acquaint ourselves with heaven, the more easily we will die. C. S. Lewis said,

> "I must keep alive in myself the desire for my true country, which I shall not find until after death. I must never let it get snowed under or turned aside. I must make it the main object of life to press onto to that other country and to help others to do the same."

We have a phenomenal future. Of all people we are most blessed.

Summary

Satisfaction

The next big issue of life that we risk pursuing independently of God is satisfaction. Daily we are faced with the choice of putting ourselves or God first. We must beware of following the world's agenda of getting satisfaction at any price which will only lead us away from God and His purposes for our lives. The rich young ruler missed out on the excitement of a life following Jesus because he was unwilling to relinquish his current lifestyle.

Identity

Many people fear letting go of the issues of their lives simply because they think they will have an identity crisis, like Susan who wondered, "If I was no longer deaf, who would I be?" But we must derive our identity from our relationship with Christ. In Him we find our true identity and sense of self-worth.

Acceptance

"Our greatest need is acceptance, our greatest fear rejection." We will do almost anything to avoid being rejected and almost anything to be accepted. We people-please or put on a bold, boasting front, or wear a mask we think is acceptable to others. But all these methods rob us of real intimacy with God and with others.

Dying to self is never easy, but we need to stop all our efforts to win these things ourselves and trust God to provide us with them.

Conclusion

Freedom is a massive subject, but I hope the previous pages have given you some small understanding of what might be holding you back from enjoying the freedom that Christ has bought for us all. However, it is not enough simply to know what is wrong. We may still need help in finding the way forward, and I hope the suggested keys have been useful in unlocking some of the doors that may have been barring the way. The challenge of getting rid of the stuff that weighs us down and prevents us enjoying the pleasures of the kingdom may seem costly, but when we begin to experience the "dance of freedom" we will know the truth of Jim Elliot's words: "He is no fool who gives what he cannot keep to gain that which he cannot lose."

So,

" ... let us throw off everything that hinders and the sin that so easily entangles, and run with perseverance the race marked out for us." (Hebrews 12:1)

We hope you enjoyed *Cry Freedom*.
This book was published in partnership with New Wine.
New Wine exists to equip local churches through training
and resources, and to establish a network of churches
founded on the same values of worship, teaching
and ministry in the power of the Holy Spirit.
To find out more, visit
www.new-wine.org

For details of other books published by New Wine
Ministries, including a range of 2,000 titles from
other Word and Spirit publishers, please visit
www.newwineministries.co.uk
or email
newwine@xalt.co.uk